Actions, Not Words

The Sermons of Rabbi I. Edward Kiev

© 2002 by Ari Kiev. All rights reserved.

No part of this book may be reproduced, stored in a retrieval system, or transmitted by any means, electronic, mechanical, photocopying, recording, or otherwise, without written permission from the author.

ISBN: 1-4033-0851-9 (e-book)
ISBN: 1-4033-0852-7 (Paperback)
ISBN: 1-4033-2983-4 (Dustjacket)

Library of Congress Control Number: 2002091301

This book is printed on acid free paper.

Printed in the United States of America
Bloomington, IN

1stBooks - rev. 08/26/02

Biographical Notes on I. Edward Kiev

Isaac Edward Kiev was born in New York City in 1905, to Nathan and Anna (Radin) Kiev. In 1923 he came to the attention of Rabbi Steven S. Wise and entered Rabbi Wise's new rabbinical seminary, the Jewish Institute of Religion. While a student, Kiev worked as a page in the *JIR library,* thus getting an early start on what was to become his career as a librarian.

He served as Assistant Librarian at the Jewish Institute of Religion under Librarians Salo W. Baron (1927-1930) and Shalom Spiegel (1930-1942). In 1942 Rabbi Kiev was named Librarian of the JIR, and he held this position until his death in 1975. He also was a chaplain at the Sea-View Hospital, a tuberculosis sanitarium, and rabbi at Congregation Habonim.

He married Mary B. Nover, on December 20, 1930. Mary shared his profession, and was the librarian at the Temple Emanu-El from 1949 until her death in 1964. They had two children, Ari and Aviva. In 1994 Ari and his wife Phyllis chose to donate Rabbi Kiev's extensive literary collection to Gelman Library.

After World War II, Rabbi Kiev actively participated in effort fostering the restoration and growth of Jewish libraries. He served as secretary to the Jewish Cultural Reconstruction, which was responsible for the inventory of Jewish artifacts after the Holocaust, from 1949 to 1951. He was president of the Jewish Librarians Association, the predecessor of the current *Association of Jewish Libraries,* from 1951 to 1959. He worked with the *Council of Archives and Research Libraries in Jewish Studies* and the Jewish

Book Council. He served as treasurer of the latter from 1954 to 1958, secretary from 1958 to 1966, and as an associate editor of the *Jewish Book Annual* from 1952 to 1975, contributing the bibliography of American non-fiction books. He was also an editor for *Library Trends* and *Studies in Bibliography and Booklore,* and a contributor to many other publications such as the *American Jewish Year Book.*

In 1956 he was awarded an honorary Doctor of Divinity degree from the *Hebrew Union College-Jewish Institute of Religion.* In his letter informing Rabbi Kiev of the honor, Nelson Glueck, the president said:

> Your devotion to the knowledge and history of our people and your meticulous care and splendid talents have contributed greatly to the building of our library to its present fine reputation. You have brought honor to our institution.

The library of the Jewish Institute of Religion had always collected modern Hebrew literature. Rabbi Kiev served as a chair of the Israel Matz fund, a foundation to support Hebrew writers. *Contemporary Authors* calls him an "expert on Judaic and Hebrew literature". In his obituary, the *New Your Times* quoted Alfred Gottschalk, the president of HUC-JIR, as saying that "generations of students and scholars were helped by his phenomenal knowledge of Jewish and general literature." His stature was such that he was listed in *Who's Who in America* (1974,1976,1978); *Who's Who in the World* (1964,1976) and *Who's Who in World Jewry* (1972).

In addition to his contributions to journals in bibliography and librarianship, he translated the *Kafra Haggadah,* and was honored in a festschrift called *Studies in Jewish bibliography, history, and literature in honor of I. Edward Kiev.* During his tenure at the JIR, the library's collection grew from under 10,000 volumes to more than 100,000. Rabbi I. Edward Kiev was truly a person in whose life books played an indispensable role. In the course of his life he assembled an extraordinary personal collection of Jewish and Hebrew books which are now housed in the Kiev Collection in the Gelman Library of George Washington University in Washington, D.C. To learn more about the Kiev collection log on to the website GWU.EDU.SPECIALCOLLECTIONS.

TABLE OF CONTENTS

Jewish Identity/Tradition 1
    Let Our Record Be Written in a Book 3
    The Miracle of Jewish Survival 4
    What Is a Jew? 8
    "Personal" Judaism 10
    Obligations of a Reform Jew 12

The Morality of Judaism 15
    Humanity 17
    Moral Law 18
    Conscience 24
    Judaism's Faith in Man 29

Love Of God 37
    The Road Not Taken 39
    Actions, Not Words 41
    Make Ye Ready the Way of the Lord 44
    Definitions 47
    Ethical Freedom 50
    Humility, Compassion, Aspiration 51
    Fellowship 53
    The Ability To Listen 56

Choice/Self-Renewal 59
    Repentance and Renewal 61
    Prayer 67

Living The Present 73
    Simple Pleasures 75
    Accept The Universe 78

Let Us Begin 87

Jewish Survival 91
Our 300-Year History 93
Religious Freedom 98
Maintaining Our Judaism 102
Yom Kippur 105
A Time For Values 106
Rosh Hashanah 107
Hanukkah 109

Thoughts Of Comfort 111
Patience 113
Death 119
Courage 122

INTRODUCTION

"In every great teacher there is an ambition to transmit the fire of his soul, the passion of his hope to his students. In every great teacher there is the capacity for human understanding and sympathy. He fulfills the primary requirement of the gentleman and the scholar- that the man be greater than his learning. And the real reason of his great influence is his personality. In the tried and tested teacher-the one who we can call *Norenu* – there are all these things and one thing more. And that one thing is mystic and intangible. It cannot be learned or imitated. It is a kind of glow that emanates from only one, and communicates itself to all."

This mystic spark of which my father spoke, the *neshama yeterah,* he himself possessed. His charisma, his sparkle, his inner peace and enthusiasm for helping others in a way which was never critical or judgmental, resulted from a unique combination of self-reliance, love of God, devotion to family and optimism about mankind and from his awareness of being the teacher-companion "who somehow has preserved gentleness of heart and serenity, one whose very presence says to us, "Yesterday was dark; tomorrow may be stormy, but today the sun is shining."

Through example my father bequeathed a legacy of a moral life endowed with noble, but attainable, ideals. His influence endures in the unending consequences flowing from his character and deeds: it endures in the lives of those who knew him; it endures in the sentiments set forth in these sermons which express his strong commitment to others.

> "In the school of life we choose our own teachers and they are the companions who build our mind and our mood. But it is of greater moral moment that as we choose, so are we chosen; and, for better or for worse, we are the teacher of others. We can only humbly hope that the influence which we exert is one of courage and calmness, so that we may obey the rabbinic word "to learn, to teach and to fulfill."

There are many vital themes he addressed himself to in his life and in his teachings. On one occasion he noted that: "The founders of Judaism understood the dangers of mere lip service to God: there are no required affirmations of faith. This is what is required: Not to believe in God but to love God."

These words, spoken in the context of one of his many inspiring sermons, characterized for my father not only the essence of Judaism but also the essence of humanity: personal fulfillment through love. Love, he believed, manifested itself in countless ways, through an indefinable on-going process, confirmed and reinforced through religious prayer and ritual.

By caring for himself and all those who had contact with him, his actions ultimately reflected his own strong love of God. Repeatedly he affirmed that the belief which is called for is belief in our own value and worth; the faith which is necessary recognizes that each individual has the capacity to choose, to repent, to improve.

There is compassion here and there is wisdom: there is inspiration, challenge and history. Many of the themes touched upon in the pages which follow transcend the confines of a given time or place, nor is their relevance limited to a particular situation. The power of love is universal; the constant striving toward improvement affects good men everywhere. The search for integrity and courage is never-ending.

At least such was the case with my father. His deep humility, along with his knowledge, were what his colleagues found most characteristic of him. His presence signified a fully reconciled heart and mind; a man at peace with himself and therefore capable of being generous to others. His manner attracted and served as a model for several generations of students from all over the world.

The violation of the rights of others, whether on a national or personal level, was probably the only thing which moved him to anger. He believed that the dignity of the individual must never be compromised, and that no power on earth could require it to be. His prayers were for peace—among nations, among families, and within ourselves.

Whether these sermons are skimmed or studied, it seems certain the reader will return to them again and again. Each reader will bring to them something unique, so too will each take something special away.

As a Rabbi my father's frame of reference was focused mainly on things Judaic. But as a scholar, teacher, and friend, his perspective was all-encompassing. Consequently, I believe that the contents of this volume will prove inspirational, comforting, and challenging to adherents of all faiths.

Ari Kiev, M.D.

Actions, Not Words

JEWISH IDENTITY/TRADITION

I. Edward Kiev

Actions, Not Words

Let Our Record Be Written in a Book

Remember us unto the purpose for which we were created: life. Inscribe us and let our record be worthy so that it be written in a book. We write our own book of life. Each of us, no matter what station in life we are at, no matter how high or low, intellectual or illiterate, creative or inarticulate, every one of us is author of a story, of a tale that is told. Many of us are co-authors of books in the making, yea the unwritten books and the books of life to come; the unwritten records of our children and their children and the generations to follow. What would we not do to get a glimpse, to see only the outline of happiness and the sorrow that the future may bring! If we could only direct and teach, warn and teach those to come to beware of the pitfalls in the way of life, in the way of a better world.

The source books of the future are being made by us. Shall we deceive the future and offer in only a civilization of gadgets, of outer comforts of life, of implements of war and destruction? Shall we betray the past and say nothing that has been bequeathed to us by the past, is worth continuing? Can we deny our past to the generations that follow us? Let us not deceive ourselves. No assimilation with other religious, no conversion to other faiths - compulsory or voluntarily - no denial of the origin and destiny of Israel, no act by any man or group within or without Israel, will deter us from our faith and hope in God and in our people.

I. Edward Kiev

Miracle of Jewish Survival

The spiritual survival of the Jew - the history of the Jewish people - is an experience which defies all of the rules of politics, economics, and sociology. We disrupt the theories of the Marxes, the Spenglers, the Toynbees of all ages. We astonish even ourselves.

According to the rules, our people should have disappeared long ago. Twenty-five hundred and seventy one years ago when the Temple of Jerusalem lay in ruins and masses of our people sat in exile in Babylon, our ancestors themselves were certain that the end had come: "We have lost all hope. We are as dry bones." And yet, a generation later, a miracle of resurrection had occurred, the astonished prophet Isaiah looking out at the reborn household of Israel exclaimed: "Who has borne me these? I had lost my children and was desolate, exiled and captive. Who hath brought up these? Behold, I was left alone. Whence, then, have these come?"

The people which had seemed dead, was reborn and renewed as if by a miracle. This miracle has since been repeated many times: It has become a pattern of the Jewish past.

Who can count the number of times that the end of our people seemed certain? In distant times and recent times our enemies rejoiced and our own people mourned in the face of what seemed to be inevitable. In the days of our grandparents, the Hebrew poet Judah Leib Gordon wrote: "Who knows but that I am the last singer of Zion and you dear reader are the last who will understand my songs."

Actions, Not Words

Long before the time of Hitler and Stalin, the combination of external persecution and internal corrosion led another poet, Leno Gordon, to conclude that Jewish life was in a state of hopeless decline, that it might soon come to an end. He called his poem "LEMI ANI OMEL," "FOR WHOM DO I LABOR." He thought he was the last.

We are here today, and the two million Jews in the land of Israel, knew how mistaken Gordon was in his apprehensions. He wasn't the last at all. In fact, he was the first, the father of a reborn Hebrew literature. He knew that at the very time that Gordon wrote his poems, the first pioneers were on their way to Palestine to establish the foundation of modern Israel, while the first great wave of Jewish immigrants were coming to America.

One epoch in Jewish history was coming to an end, but a renaissance, an era of new birth was taking place. New centers of Jewish life were incubating. The seeds of new and flourishing communities were being planted. Even after the great losses of the Hitler holocaust, the people of Israel continued to live and thrive. This time the miracle of Jewish survival is sustained, not in the past but in the present. We, all of us together, and our children and children's children represent and embody the latest miracle of Jewish survival.

As a result of this special experience of ours, we are equipped with special gifts and capacities. How else shall we explain the unique achievement of our people? Why, then, have the children of Israel been so blessed?

I. Edward Kiev

There is nothing special about the Jewish people except their tradition. This tradition, both the ideals of Judaism and the actual experience of the Jewish people, is what makes the difference. It is this tradition, with its emphasis on deeds and actions, on man's ability to know what is good and to do it, that has nourished ideals and commitment to humanitarian causes among Jews. It is Jewish culture with its broad view of history and experience which opened minds and broadened horizons. It is the social pattern of Jewish life with emphasis on learning and responsibility which has developed the character and the intellect of the Jewish people.

It is the role of the Jewish people in society, as a minority, as underdog, frequently as the nonconformist opposed to coercion, which has developed our desire for autonomy and individualism. Sigmund Freud said he was able to expound his new theories because being a Jew taught him how to live in opposition – the DAVKA attitude – that too is part of the tradition.

That is the secret: our tradition. We are beneficiaries of a marvelous heritage. Our past casts light into our present and each day we are reaping and replacing a rich harvest of achievement, in every area except one.

The one area where we seem to be slowing down is in the renewing of the tradition itself. American Jewry, which has achieved such fantastic success in so many ways, seems to be failing in securing its own survival. The failure is as obvious as the success. We have carelessly squandered our heritage. We are using the capital of our great inheritance, our primary resource, without adding to it or replacing it.

Actions, Not Words

The result is that at the very moment when our legacy is stimulating remarkable creativity, we witness a steady decline in Jewish knowledge, in Jewish practice, and less and less commitment to our spiritual heritage and tradition. Side by side with the old strengths which we still have, there are signs of many weaknesses.

Looking critically at ourselves today, we sometimes wonder, *Is American Jewry to vanish?*

It is our destiny to live for our children's sake, for mankind's sake, for God's sake, to live and continue to represent a miracle of spirit over circumstances, as befits the marvelous and mysterious people of Israel. This is the challenge which all the revivals of the past present to us. Let us pledge to rebuild our life, to renew it and to enrich it, so that we may be rebuilt and enriched with God's blessing. Then we shall not be the last, but the first, the beginners of new life and new strength for the life of our people.

I. Edward Kiev

WHAT IS A JEW?

I have often asked myself whether there is a satisfactory definition of a Jew. The word signifies, to be sure, an individual belonging to a people that has endured for many centuries. It is found in the good and bad literature of the nations. Beginning with the Bible and appearing in endless quantities of books, the name Jew, like the person of the Jew, has continued to arouse the curiosity, the loyalty, the passion, the sentiment, the revulsion and the bafflement of people everywhere. It has been extolled and it has been condemned, defended and attacked. The fact that the Jew has lived in many countries and climes; in many periods of history under many trials and tribulations with varying degrees of fortune, is in itself sufficient to stir the imagination concerning his identity. The poet Heinrich Heine, a Jew himself, considered the Jew a curse. The Christian Counsellor to Frederick the Great considered him a miracle. Definitions become confusing in the light of conflicting interests and loyalties the Jews themselves pursue. Some call themselves members of a religious community. Others claim status as members of a social group. Some considered themselves secularists while others call themselves sectarians. Some are mystic and some are rationalists. Some are believing and others are unbelieving individuals. But all have this in common, it would seem: They're members of a group held together by physical bonds resulting from birth. They may add to the content of their physical existence and intensify their consciousness as Jews or they may not. Whether they move in the currents of organized Jewish life or remain on the periphery, they are all subject to a common fate and destiny. Since it is the idea that lends distinction to a group and is bound up with its physical existence, we look for a definition of the Jew in terms of the ideas he represents.

Tolstoy said the Jew is that sacred being who has brought down from heaven that everlasting fire, and has illumed with it the entire world. He is the religious source, spring and fountain out of which all the rest of the people have drawn their beliefs and their religions.

The Jew is the pioneer of liberty and the pioneer of civilization. The Jew is the emblem of civil and religious tolerance. The Jew is the emblems of eternity.

Jewishness is the Jewish way of looking at things. More precisely, it is the universal spirit as it is embodied in the Jewish soul.

Jewishness is that which enables the Jews, in time of national independence, to build institutions as an embodiment of their creative will. Jewishness is, especially in such times, joy, ecstasy, zestful living.

I. Edward Kiev

"PERSONAL" JUDIASM

I would begin my sermon to you this Yom Kippur day by reciting a story concerning the famous Rabbi Israel *Baal Shem Tov*. When the Baal Shem Tov had a difficult task before him, he would go to a certain place in the woods, light a fire and meditate in prayer. When a generation later a Jew was faced with a similar task, he would go to that same place in the woods and say "I can no longer light a fire, but I can still speak a prayer."

But a generation later, facing the same task, a Jew went into the woods and said: I can no longer light a fire, nor do I know the meaning of prayer, but I know the place in the woods to which it belongs, and that is sufficient." And when still another generation had passed, and a Jew was confronted with a similar task he remained where he was and said, "I cannot light the fire, I cannot speak the prayer, I do not know the place, but I can tell the tale of how it was done."

This is a choice parable describing the deterioration of a vital religious experience. What was for the Baal Shem an experience of intense religious fervor, became later just a tale to be told.

We are Jews, as we are men and women. The alternative to our existence as Jews is spiritual suicide, disappearance. It is not a change into something else. Judaism has allies but not substitutes. Every people has a religion that it has received from others. Only the Jews have learned that people and Torah are united as one with God. All of Israel, not only the select few, are the bearers of this great unity.

Actions, Not Words

Much has been spoken and written in our time about nation and society, about the community and its institutions. But the individual has been lost sight of. It is common knowledge that Judaism is not merely concerned with the individual. He who goes his own way, abandons the Jewish way. To withdraw oneself from the community is to detach oneself from the God of Israel. However, it is a fact that the Jewish people today are like a tree from which many fruits are falling off.

What was the situation of the Jews before the time of emancipations? As an individual he was able to preserve his spiritual privacy. His life had form, direction, inner strength and dignity. He stood for eternity, he lived for a transcendent purpose. It was the collective existence of the Jews that was in danger. Recognizing the distress of the Jews as a people was the great achievement of Moses Hess, and Pinaker, and Herzl who thought about this problem which culminated in the Zionist movement.

I. Edward Kiev

REFORM JEW'S OBLIGATIONS

First is the obligation to *study,* to know the essentials of Jewish teachings. This is particularly incumbent upon reform Jews who in order to winnow the chaff from the wheat must know the beliefs of our faith which have relevance and authenticity for our times. Liberal Jews have no license to be ignorant; on the contrary, they must understand the historical development of Judaism in order to understand how our faith came about. They should be well versed in history and literature of Judaism so that they can distill the essence of its teaching and recognize the ethical imperatives that govern our code of conduct. The Talmud was never more correct when it taught "An ignorant man cannot be pious."

Second is the obligation to *pray,* not to ourselves as a form of auto-suggestion, but to God. We need as never before to seek God's inspiration and God's guidance for the hectic times we live in. Nowadays we move at such a dizzy pace that we require personal quietude for meditation not just when it is convenient, but regularly to gather together in kinship with others and seek Divine guidance for the decisions of life.

Third is the obligation to *practice* the *ethical life,* to "do justly and love mercy and walk humbly with God." Strange. Strange as it may seem it is even harder for us than it was for the very orthodox Jews. Anyone can follow the rules and regulations laid down by the Shalhan Amik. It is much harder to be selective, to be informed, to decide for oneself on the basis of reading and study and guidance what to retain, what to practice, and what to refashion.

Actions, Not Words

It seems as if all that Americans of any of the three major religions want to get out of their faith are primarily, "peace of mind, happiness, success, and worldly achievement." Prosperity, success and advancement in business become obvious ends for which religion, or rather the religious attitude of believing, are held to be useful. Religion is expected to produce a kind of spiritual euphoria, a sense of well being and buoyancy, that comfortable feeling that one is all right with God. One theologian, Roy Echkhardt calls this the cult of divine-human chumminess, in which God is envisaged...as the friendly neighbor who is always ready to give you the friendly pat on the back you need when you happen to feel blue."

So in other words, what Americans seem to expect from this revival of religion is peace of mind that will conquer insecurity and anxiety, overcome inner conflict, shed guilt and fear, and make everyone normal and well adjusted. In short, religion is expected to be a spiritual anodyne, a soothing syrup designed to allay pains and assuage the vexations of existence. Note well that in this kind of religion, so naively man centered, not God-centered, it is not man who serves God but God who is mobilized and made to serve man and his purposes whether these purposes be economic prosperity, free enterprises, social reform, democracy, happiness, security, or peace of mind.

I. Edward Kiev

Actions, Not Words

THE MORALITY OF JUDAISM

I. Edward Kiev

HUMANITY

There is nothing more important about a person than his opinion of humanity. From this flows all conduct. If it be high, his actions will be humane and humanitarian: if it be high, his actions will be full of so-called human errors and mistakes. Rabbi Ben Azzai realized that one's philosophy of humanity is the most important fact about him. Let him believe he is only human, he will behave as such. Let him believe that to be human is to be divine, he will be divine. I say to you, tell me what a man thinks of creation, of humanity, or the ideals fostered by our faith and I will tell you his life, his deeds, his value to society, and his capacity for justice, honor, mercy and love.

I. Edward Kiev

MORAL LAW

Our age is distraught, and not because its high hopes for scientific progress have not been realized. It is because it has failed to give man what he hoped for and what he needs pre-eminently – security, dignity, happiness. He had come to believe that his scientific laboratories held for him the magic key to all progress well-being, but in the darkening and threatening world in which he now finds himself, he cries unto these helpless idols, like the priest of BAAL in the name of Elijah, "O BAAL, answer us." But "though they proceeded to slash one another according to their custom with swords and lances until the blood gushed out upon them….there was no voice, nor answer." Our age is suffering from what the Bible calls "the drooping of the soul," a dangerous definition of morale, a spiritual malaise. Its brilliant intellectual and scientific achievements only make phosphorescent the appalling stages of decomposition.

Prophetic religion admonished man to replace reverence for the moral law above all knowledge, and urged men to find therein their security, dignity and happiness. Knowledge is important. It, too, is of God. Knowledge expands and enriches life. It opens up new continents for the adventuring spirit of man. But "the beginning of knowledge is reverence for God."

In God, human life finds meaning. The mission of Judaism is to help men find meaning in a universe where ultimate meaning is forever hidden from there. Albert Einstein writes, "What is the meaning of human life, or of organic life altogether? To answer this question at all implies a religion. Is there any sense then, you ask, in posing it? I answer, the man who regards his own life and that of his fellow creatures as meaningless is not merely unfortunate but almost disqualified for life."

There was a time when scientists were confident that they would soon work out the solution for the riddle of the universe. It was only a matter of time, they thought, only a matter of probing deeper and deeper, of adding one fact to another, one discovery to another, until the required total was reached, before men would know all they wished to know.

In our generation scientists are less confident. The most erudite among them today acknowledge that "In the evolution of scientific thought, one fact has become impressively clear: There is no mystery of the physical world which does not point to a mystery beyond itself. For man is enchained by the very condition of his being, his finiteness. ...Man is his own greatest mystery."

Although man has been denied the knowledge of objective reality – the how and why of things – he is nevertheless permitted to learn the relations between things and forces which exist in the universe. While he may never be able to completely understand the nature and origin of electricity or gravitation or magnetism, he may come to understand their effect, and thus be able to use them to his advantage, to increase his power and his security in the world. It is through unlimited research and investigation into the relationships of things and forces, in learning how things operate and how we can use them, that man can find great rewards and abundant satisfactions. Thus, even though our scientific knowledge may never be

I. Edward Kiev

absolute, it nevertheless offers a world of enterprise, challenge and meaning to satisfy a purposeful and victorious life.

That is true also of man's spiritual life. We can never learn the nature of God, nor can we ever understand the ultimate purpose of creation. The great religious thinkers were the first to point this out, and stressed in time and again. Nevertheless, man has not been left in utter darkness concerning those matter which affect his moral destiny in this unknowable universe. Much has been made known to us through seers and prophets, as well as by our own experience. Therefore, we are able to recognize God's laws of justice, love, truth and selflessness in the world of men; and living by these laws, we may prosper.

In one of his essays, Bertrand Russell wrote: "The importance of man, which is the one indispensable dogma of the theologians, receives no support from a scientific view of the future of the solar system." But time and again, science has been tardy in arriving at conclusions which the intuitive religious genius of mankind postulated long ago. Furthermore, there are religious convictions which require no confirmation at the hands of science.

Both Judaism and Christianity hold that man has immense significance in the scheme of things. Each man, rich or poor, simple or wise, black or white, saint or sinner, is important to God in the unfoldment of His purpose. Man should live and act as if his life were tremendously significant, as if he were a co-worker of God.

The universal moral law which Judaism proclaims demands much of man in terms of duty and sacrifice,

Actions, Not Words

but it gives much to him in terms of high and independent status, dignity and inalienable rights. "Every man has the right to say, for my sake the world was created."

One of the sages of Israel, long ago, employing the rich imaginative style which so often characterized their utterances, declared: "When a man goes forth on his way, a troop of angels precede him and proclaim: "Make way for the image of God, blessed be He."

The immortal mandate of Scripture, "Thou shall love thy neighbor as thyself," come as climax and summation of a serious of prescriptions and ordinances intended to stress reverence for human life and respect for the personality of every individual. "Thou shall not oppress thy neighbor...thou shall not curse the deaf, nor put a stumbling block before the blind...thou shalt not respect the person of the poor, nor favor the person of the might; but in righteousness shall thou judge thy neighbor...thou shall not spread false reports among thy people...thou shall not hate thy brother in thy heart...thou shall not take vengeance nor be intolerant of thy fellowmen."

Our age, unfortunately, puts little emphasis on the individual. Men are handled impersonally in the mass. Increasingly, they are becoming statistics. They are born by the millions and they are slaughtered by the millions. Because the religious basis of our society has been denied, replaced by materialistic theories of life and history, the stature of the individual, and with it, his rights and inherent dignity, have suffered tragic abatement and diminution in our day. Every precinct of his life is invaded and violated. The most endangered person in the world today is the man who thinks for

I. Edward Kiev

himself. The eagerly awaited "people's century" has not brought with it individual freedom.

Our age has rejected substance as well as the methodology of prophetic religion, yet one of its essential contributions has been the concept of method. There is not only God and the good life, there is also the way – the good way – the only way which leads to the good life. Judaism defined a method by which men might attain morally desirable ends, a method worthy of the ends. It outlaws the notion that moral ends justify immoral means. Each step toward the realization of a worthy objective must be a worthy objective itself. Means have a way of inserting and integrating themselves into ends, even of determining their ultimate pattern. Therefore, to establish justice or freedom or peace, the ways of justice, freedom, and peace must be employed. There is no justice without love: on the basis of justice alone the world cannot endure.

Judaism does not ask the impossible of man. It does not set goals which are forever beyond his reach. "This commandment which I command this day, is not too hard for thee, neither is it far off. It is not in heaven...neither is it beyond the sea, but the word is very nigh unto thee, in thy mouth, in thy heart, that thou mayest do it." It does not reject this world wherein man could not fulfill himself. It does not deny us our normal enjoyments or summon us to self-mortification or asceticism.

It does not regard any human institution, sacred or secular, as infallible, nor any governmental system as flawless or adequate insurance against abuse of power, the exploitation of man, and the defeat of the spiritual

Actions, Not Words

promises of human life. It warns of the moral pitfalls hidden in every form of excess, even in the excess of virtue, and in every political or economic system. It admonishes men not to make the works of their hands their God.

The method which Judaism carefully defines, calls for the acceptance of the moral law of justice tempered by love, which is binding on all of us at all times, individually and collectively. "The good way" calls for the curbing of unlimited power, and a rejection of irresponsible authority. No one is above the moral law.

The classic way of Judaism has never been fully tried. The time has come to "Make you a new heart and a new spirit: for why will ye die, O house of Israel…Turn yourselves and live."

I. Edward Kiev

CONSCIENCE

When a man of his own accord seeks to submit to a scrutiny of his heart, when he voluntarily prays for a thorough examination of his mind and spirit, of his thoughts and conduct, it is a sign that he has reached a very high level of morality. For the contrary course is what we usually meet with; as a rule, men wish to conceal what is really in their hearts, and to hide whatever evil and wrong they may have been guilty of, and to appear better and fairer than they really are.

It is the merit of Yom Kippur that it would stimulate each one of us in the direction of the Psalmist's course, to repeat the prayer: "Teach me O God, and know my heart: try me and know my thoughts: and see if there be any wickedness in me." Its purpose is to make us see ourselves as we really are, to hold the mirror up to our inward nature, to remove for once every mark and outward cover, and have us stand before our own selves and the eye of God in the actuality of our character and conduct.

It would even make us eager for a scrutiny of our heart and a thorough examination of our conscience, much as a merchant, who for some time has carried on his business without conscientious bookkeeping, might of a sudden be overcome with a desire to know the whole truth about his business, and be rid, once and for all, of uncertainty and guesswork. And insofar as the Day of Atonement seeks to do this, even if it does not wholly succeed, it cannot but be welcomed by every man or woman interested in his own moral improvement as well as in the ethical progress of the world.

Actions, Not Words

For there can be no moral progress, either for the individual or the world at large, without an improvement in and refinement of conscience. The surest indication of the moral status of an age or country lies in the condition of its conscience – the degree of its vitality or callousness- its apathy or keenness - the sort of things it would sanction or condemn. We need not enter now into a discussion of whether the conscience of the modern world is superior to that of former times. Whether or not one believes this, it seems that whoever is familiar with the trends of modern life will not deny that there is much room for improvement. Indeed, the conscience of today still requires much refinement, not to say awakening, and still requires an infusion of greater energy and vitality, if we are to have real progress in human conduct, in social well-being and happiness.

Our conscience represents several aspects or sides which are not always of the same moral quality. It is not always a moral until acting with equal certainty and equal goodness on all questions. Rather, it often seems to offer the spectacle of being divided into many compartments, differing radically one from another in the views and sentiments they harbor. But real moral progress we shall never have, and never will our conduct develop into the chief architect of the world's happiness, until the conscience of men has been unified to always respond with understanding, keenness, and energy.

What, then, are some of the phases of conscience?

There is the individual, or personal conscience – the private conscience, you might call it. We cannot fail to agree that the private conscience of the

I. Edward Kiev

individual is not only the basis of all character, but also the foundation of all happiness in the world. All the business of life depends first on all the direct personal contact of a man with man; everything else comes next. The question is what sort of conscience a man carries about with him in his private life, in his direct personal contact with other human beings, in his daily coming and going? Let a man be ever so great a figure on the stage of the world, if on the matter of those private contacts and private obligations his heart is old and his conscience asleep or deficient, he is sure to be the cause of a great deal of evil and unhappiness. And how often do we hear of such men: the successful businessman playing a big role in his factory or store, but a veritable tyrant in the treatment of his subordinates; the great artist or statesman sizzling his associates with his brilliant talent but devoid of all consideration or decency in his relation to his wife and child; the man of the world, known to his friends as hail-fellow-well-met, boon companion and generous spender, and yet dead to all sentiments of kindness and chivalry toward his own mother and sister. The world is full of instances of this sort, and never will the world be a happy place, nor a moral place, until this individual conscience, this private side of human conscience, has experienced an awakening and refinement.

In addition, there is what we frequently call the social conscience, that side of conscience which influences our relations to society at large.

Finally there is the universal, the human, the cosmic conscience.

Actions, Not Words

How can we achieve a revitalization of our "conscience"?

First, by scrutiny. The reason why conscience so often dies is that we are not in the habit of subjecting our own actions and thoughts to careful examination. There is many a man who has lost his character not so much because he was bad, but because he was thoughtless. He never really stopped to examine his own life, to inspect his own heart, to take a look into his conscience. Yom Kippur is a day for the scrutiny of one's own self, which is the first step in the education of the conscience.

Secondly, by determination to improve. The watchword of Yom Kippur is not only forgiveness, but improvement. Our learned teachers said: "One must not come before the Almighty from Atonement Day to Atonement Day with the same bundle of sins. The same sins are not forgiven successively." What they meant is that the Yom Kippur service and spirit is in vain unless from year to year it registers a real desire for improvement, a real desire to advance in one's moral perception and practice.

And, finally, by the possession of an ideal – the aspiration toward standard of moral life. We hear a great deal of talk about people who claim they follow their conscience. But let us not forget that conscience itself needs guidance and inspiration, or it may deteriorate and forfeit all its power. It was Nathaniel Hawthorne who pointed out that conscience is a coward, and the things which it is not strong enough to prevent, it often lacks the courage to condemn and finally learns to condone. Let us be sure, then, that in our effort to educate and refine our conscience we have

I. Edward Kiev

some ideal to set before it, and that the ideal is the highest within reach.

JUDAISM'S FAITH IN MAN

There are certain key words in the language of all cultures which signify their quintessence, in a phrase, in a word, or even in a song. Americans jointly possess such concepts as *democracy, majority rule, freedom of speech.* These point to the values of a civilization. There are over 200 such concepts in Judaism, terms pointing to the ideals and values of our faith. One of these is *TESHUVA.*

Teshuva is not merely an act of asking forgiveness, although its technical translation is *repentance.* But as with all value concepts, it is beyond definition. One could write a book about democracy, and maybe the reader would get the idea of what it means. But it takes the time and effort of immersing oneself in a culture or civilization to fathom its value concepts. No simple definitions are accurate or even helpful.

The next best way to understand Teshuva is to try to define what it implies. What are the cluster of Jewish values which constitute the underpinnings of Jewish theology, that can help define the concept of repentance?

The assumption is that man is a constantly improving being. He is flexible enough to overcome past weaknesses. He is courageous enough to combat former mistakes, inadequacies and unfortunate mishaps in his life. In the phrase used by the civil rights movement, he can *overcome.* In fact, one way of stating the meaning of Teshuva is "We shall overcome." There are many sayings in the English language, as in all languages, which spawn a pessimistic view of the nature of man: "You can't teach an old dog new tricks." Or, "you can't change human nature," Once a fool always a fool." These expressions imply the opposite of Teshuva. For if Teshuva implies anything, it is that mankind must have a deep faith in itself. Teshuva means that you *can* teach an old person new interests, that you *can* improve human character, and that once a fool, perhaps tomorrow a wiser man.

Teshuva means that God created basically a good world, and that man is basically a good creature. His propensities are for good. He can err, he can slip, he can backslide. But he has within himself a built-in corrective system known as conscience. He has within him a Divinely-given urge to strive upward, to climb higher, to achieve more, and to become better. These are the elements of Teshuva.

In short, Jewish theology has faith in man. The command to repent, to change, to practice Teshuva, all assume that man has the ability to effect these changes. Let none of us shortchange his own supply of faith in himself, in his family, his friends, so that he cannot bring himself to Teshuva.

Rosh Hashanah, the anniversary of creation. A time to hold up a moral mirror to our lives. What, then, shall we say about man on this day of judgment? In what light shall we see ourselves? We have heard the voices of others, of philosophers, of writers, of theologians and historians. What, pray tell, is the voice of synagogue?

Judaism believes in the reality of sin: Ours is no Pollyanna religion, deaf to the eerie and dissonant sounds of life, blind to the seamier sides of our

Actions, Not Words

existence. The pages of our Bible abound in God's summons to man and in man's failure to answer. Did not Adam disobey God's will? Did not Cain slay his brothers? Did not the children of Israel again and again thanklessly murmur against their deliverer and yearn for the fleshpots of Egypt?

The human problem has nowhere been stated more forcefully than by the prophet Isaiah more than 2500 years ago: "Thus said the Lord, why, when I came, was there no man; when I called was there no one to answer?"

What is man? He is a creature endowed with the freedom to say "no" to his Creator. He is a creature who can and often does abuse the power which God has given him. *Man is capable of great evil.* This is part of Judaism's image of man – but only part!

For Freedom is a two-edged sword. If God has given man the power to brutalize life, he has also given him the power to sanctify it. And so, let us ask again, what is the Jewish view of man?

Many centuries ago, Rabbi Jose of Galilee sat in the academy and addressed himself to this very question. In the presence of student and colleagues, he said" "There are three kinds of man; the righteous or saintly are those whose life appears to be governed by their Yezer Tov[1], the wicked are governed by their Yezer Ra[2]," and then he added: "There is a middle category."

If pressed to illustrate his example, Rabbi Jose might well have said Abraham is an example of the

---

[1] Inclination toward good
[2] evil inclination

righteous, and Haman an example of the wicked. If he were alive today, Rabbi Jose might have substituted the names of Leo Baeck or Martin Buber as righteous men, and Adolf Eichmann as wicked.

But what of the middle category? Whom does that embrace? Rabba, a Babylonian rabbi, answers that question on the very same page of the Talmud. Said Rabba, "We are his middle category." The average person is neither righteous nor wicked. We are both perpetrators of sin and pursuers of the good.

Is this not more an authentic image of our own lives than that purveyed by the current hucksters of despair in literature, on Broadway and off-Broadway, in art and on the platform? We are neither depraved nor saintly. Each of us is witness to a personal struggle between integrity and expediency, compassion and insensitivity, love and hate, noble self-giving, and petty self-seeking. Our soul is the battleground between good and evil. As we survey the year that has passed, do we not find victories as well as defeats?

The Jewish image of man not only aptly describes us, it addresses itself to us: Remember, O man, that you are neither blameless saint nor incorrigible sinner. Be then not overly wicked in your own eyes. Remember, O man, you are probably not as worthless as you sometimes think you are. You have, no doubt, succumbed at times to the evil inclination, but think- have you not also performed acts of redemptive kindness?

Remember, O man, short of the Messianic age, there are no ultimate victories in our moral life, but neither are our defeats irrevocable. It is easy to lapse

Actions, Not Words

from a posture of righteousness but it is also possible to return unto the Lord, your God.

Ever regard yourself, O man, as half-guilty, and half-worthy, and weigh each of your future acts as if it might tip the moral balance of your life.

Here is the balanced mirror which Judaism would hold up to our lives. Here is the perspective in which to judge ourselves on this day of judgment. Here also is the perspective in which to judge our fellow men.

There is a legend in our tradition about a man who so despaired of his friends that he left the world of creatures and set out for the realm of mystery. When he came unto the heavenly place, he knocked. From within came the cry, "What do you want here?" The man answered, "I have proclaimed your praise to the ears of mortals but they were deaf to me, so I came to you that you yourself may hear me." From God's heavenly throne came this reply: "Turn back, I have no ear for you, I have given man the power to hear my commandments and to do them."

In this same spirit, a Jewish sage once counseled his people that there is a time when haughtiness is a duty. And when is that? "When the evil inclination approaches whispering, 'You are not worthy to fulfill the Torah'- then answer haughtily, 'I am worthy.'"

We live in an age when man's image is sorely tarnished. What can we offer in defense of the faith of our fathers? We can offer, dear friends, the testimonies of our individual lives.

Are there not many men and women here today who have witnessed, and even benefited from, the surpassing goodness of another human being? It may have come as a tender surprise or a dramatic

I. Edward Kiev

revelation; at such times, have you not found yourself saying, "My – it's enough to restore one's faith in human nature!"?

What a momentous year this would be in your life if even one person's faith in many were saved by your conduct – if through your own resistance to expediency, your own acts of sacrificial love, your offering of solace and compassion, your pursuit of truth and righteousness, you rekindled in even one soul faith in man's power to be a fallible but faithful servant of God! O, what an entry this would make in the book of our life.

There is really one story in the world, and only one; less flashy than headlines and rarely recorded in the impressive chronicles of history, it is the story of an individual man fighting a continuous battle within the depths of his soul. It is the story of man – stumbling, bungling, and fumbling – but finally triumphing over temptation, committing acts of redemptive loveliness, and vindicating an age-old faith in his moral power and promise.

One of the most powerful forces that act on every one of us is the image of ourselves that we carry around with us inside of our heads in our imaginations. That's why we call it imagination – that's the part of our mind that furnishes images for us to look at.

The chief handicap that many people have is not a poor brain, but the wrong picture of themselves, which come to dominate them. For instance, many a man is paralyzed in his actions because he has a negative image of himself as a person who can't do things and the image prevents him from putting forth a real effort.

Actions, Not Words

A wise man said, "We tend to become what we imagine ourselves to be." That is true. A track coach once made a pole vault man put in his room a picture of himself clearing the bar in fine form, not because he wanted the man to become conceited, but because he knew that the deciding factor in the man's performance would be the idea in the man's mind of what he could do. He wanted to make a positive image of the man doing a successful job dominant in the man's mind. And it worked.

One of the biggest things our forefather Abraham did was to break up negative images people had of themselves and substitute positive images. He was both an image-maker and an image-breaker.

You are a son of God. You are more than a collection of animal sensations. You can live up to the level of the new image of yourself, which is the true one.

I. Edward Kiev

Actions, Not Words

LOVE OF GOD

I. Edward Kiev

Actions, Not Words

THE ROAD NOT TAKEN

While we pray and hope for life, we are all mindful of the perils and uncertainties of Life. The very spelling of the word calls attention to the vast contingencies with which life is fraught. In the very middle of the word LIFE, there is IF. In the middle of every life there is a big I F.

Robert Frost made this point sharply in a haunting little poem called "The Road Not Taken." Once while walking through the forest he came upon a fork where two paths branched out. Naturally, he could take only one but in the poem he wonders what would have happened had he taken the other path.

> I shall be telling with a sigh
> Somewhere ages and ages hence
> Two roads diverged in a wood, and I
> Took the one less traveled by
> And that has made all the difference.

A man chooses a road that leads to a career or to the selection of a life's partner or to a crucial decision in his business and then in an introspective moment he thinks of the "road not taken." What would have happened if I had taken the other road? How vastly different my life might be today!

The famous artist Whistler had his heart set upon a career in the army but he was dropped from West Point because he failed in chemistry. In later life, he used to say, "If silicon had been a gas, I should have been a general."

I. Edward Kiev

Yes, the big "IF" is in the middle of every life. How often do you and I speculate about the road not taken?

The pupil of the great Chafetz Chayim had ventured forth from the Yeshiva and went far away, and prospered in business and in all his affairs. Some years later the famous rabbi passed through the city and naturally the businessman paid a visit to his great teacher.

"What are you doing?" the rabbi asked solicitously.

"Thank you," he answered, "I am doing quite well, my business has grown, I have many people working for me, I have a high financial rating." Then the conversation turned to other matters. In a little while the rabbi asked again: "What are you doing?" It seemed strange that the rabbi should repeat the question he had already answered. But the rabbi was growing older. His memory apparently was not what it used to be.

ACTIONS, NOT WORDS

A number of years ago a brilliant author and sharp analyst of human events named George Orwell wrote a very frightening book entitled *1984*. In it, he described a nightmarish, dehumanized, totalitarian world. The slogan of the government was: War is peace/Freedom is slavery/Ignorance is strength.

Orwell wrote this book to warn us of the ominous tendencies he observed in today's society. The slogans pointed up a grave danger – the danger of manipulation of language, through which our most precious words lose their meaning. Orwell was alarmingly perceptive. Today's totalitarian tyrannies call themselves "people's democracies"; the exploders of hundred megaton bombs of themselves as seeking peace.

As in political life, in religious life, too, words become increasingly empty. It is regrettable but undeniable that the statement "I believe in God" has become almost meaningless. In response to the question "Do you believe in God?" 94 per cent of Americans answer "Yes." "Does this belief affect your daily life?" and 75 percent answer "No."

Nearly everyone says "I believe in God." Even Adolph Eichmann said it. In all too many cases the statement has no meaning. In the words of the prophet Jeremiah, God "is near in their mouths and far away in their hearts."

The founders of Judaism understood the dangers of mere lip service to God, because the religion they created places little emphasis on belief. There is little theological speculation in Judaism and there are no required affirmations of faith. The relationship to God

I. Edward Kiev

emphasized in Judaism stresses something else – love of God. This is what is required: Not to "believe" in God, but to love God.

The Torah spells out what love of God means. It is not esoteric, it is not mystical or metaphysical. It is not for saints or rabbis alone. Love of God means "to walk in His ways, to keep His commandments, His statutes and ordinances." To do this "with all your heart, with all your soul, and all your might. When you sit in your house, when you walk on the way, when you rise up or when you lie down. You shall teach these commandments to your children, and shall wear them proudly as a badge." This is what love of God means in Judaism. If there is any uncertainty as to how these commandments should manifest themselves in daily practice, the prophets clarify with specific examples.

Love of God, Isaiah teaches, means "loose the fetters of wickedness, undo the bands of the yoke, let the oppressed go free, break every yoke." If you love God, "Deal your bread to the hungry and bring the poor that are cast out into your house; when you see the naked cover him." If you love God, "Do not hide yourself from your own flesh." Do not look the other way when men are in need or when injustice is done." The Torah states, "When you reap the harvest, you must leave the corners of the field and the fallen grain to the poor and the strangers in your midst."

If this is what love of God means, then each of us who considers himself religious must ask himself, "Have I loved God in my life? Have I given of my means and strength to help my brothers who are homeless and naked and hungry, or have I turned my back on them? Have I left a few gleanings of my

Actions, Not Words

harvest to good causes and charities to help the blind and the deaf and the aged and the infirm? Or have I left an afflicted soul unsatisfied?

Some of us have loved God a little, some not at all. None of us have loved God enough. None of us has loved God "with all our hearts and all our soul and all our might." If we are sensitive and aware of our failure, we experience a sense of guilt. Our tradition expects us to feel guilt about clear-cut shortcomings. At the same time, we are reminded that guilt is not the end. Guilt in Judaism is expected to be the fuel for action. It is a way station on the road to good deeds. The ultimate goal for man is reconciliation and revitalized love of God. Above the din of a world wherein there is too much strife and war, answer us with the still voice of Thy spirit:

If our lives have become shallow, deepen them.
If our principles have become shabby, repair them.
If our ideals have become tarnished, restore them.
If our hopes have become faded, revive them.
If our loyalties have grown dim, brighten them.
If our values have become confused, clarify them.
If our purposes have become blurred, sharpen them.
If our horizons have become contracted, widen them.

I. Edward Kiev

MAKE YE READY THE WAY OF THE LORD

We are living in the closing hours of an age of demolition. The "Brave New World' which men like Aldous Huxley were promising us a few short years ago has proved to be a graveyard of many of the highest hopes of mankind.

One of our philosophers recently met with an Indian sage, and during their conversation the philosopher spoke admiringly of some of the technical marvels of our generation. "Yes," replied the sage, "you can fly through the air like birds and swim in the sea like fishes, but how to walk upon earth you do not yet know." Famine, civil wars, and urban decay are but symptoms and symbols which represent the accents and accompaniments of the failure of man. They proclaim the inadequacy of all human devices and the blighting effects of man's brilliant uninspired technological breath. They reveal the sad and sorry plight of a society which is for the most part rebuked but still unrepentant by God's judgment. Human ingenuity has managed to make a neighborhood of the world; but a neighborhood unillumined by spiritual light, without brotherhood, is hell! At its very best, it is a community of conflict and confusion.

Man has failed because with a technological mind but an unregenerate heart, he has forgotten the divine order of the world. Long before he assaulted his neighbor across some national boundary, he was in revolt against his Creator. Long before he waged war against his brother, he was in rebellion against his Father and King. And until this rebellion against God is ended, until men and nations become penitent and seek forgiveness, confessing their own instead of their neighbor's sins, there can be no real and lasting peace.

Man's place in this world is to serve as an example of God's love, that he may be the instrument of the Divine purpose. Kedoshim to you. Ye shall be holy. Ye shall be perfect. To be thus is to be the kind of man or woman God intended us to be. Our forefathers understood this, our prophets understood this, ancient and modern martyrs understood this. Thus the highest form of devotion to God was universally acclaimed as Kiddush Hashem.

To be sure, man cannot create freedom, peace, fellowship and happiness. Only God can do that. But man can cooperate with God in achieving the noble ideals taught by our faith: Thou shalt Love the Lord thy God, Thou shalt Love thy neighbor as thyself. Thus, the prophetic call is again heard by all of us: "Make ye ready for the way of the Lord."

In the midst of a world broken and divided by all manner of passion and prejudice, we may be voices crying in the desert. Nevertheless we determinedly pray and re-echo the command of Isaiah, *Make ye ready the way of the Lord.*

And the place in which we can all begin is in the home, the temple, the school, the social circle, and the community. In everyday relationships and not in some distant capital are where the raw materials of either a united or divided world are to be found. Fears, prejudices, jealousies, misunderstandings, lack of appreciation – these are the sources and the poisons out of which even global wars are brewed. Where we live,

I. Edward Kiev

where we work, where we worship – let us begin our quest for perfection there.

DEFINITIONS

From the time of Spinoza on there have arisen in each generation individuals or groups who have decided for reasons of semantic clarity that God should be dropped from the vocabulary. None of the attempts have succeeded and it might be a good lesson for us to know why they failed.

In the first place, most folks are not concerned with semantics. Few of us use words in accordance with their strict definition which is found in the dictionary. Words stir the imagination and provoke images and feelings rather than neatly boxed concepts. Thus, when we use the term Uncle Sam or John Bull we may have a variety of notions about America or England but the term nonetheless serves its purpose. It encompasses a whole complex of attributes which we would have to spell out if we were giving an exact description of either country.

Evocative words give a dimension of depth as well as color to our meaning – they indicate something of how we feel about the thing or person described. By dropping such words it would be going back to a two-dimensional flat surface – one tight, self-contained little fact – rather than conveying a cluster of images and feelings.

Suppose the editors and compilers of the Bible had been infected by this itch for semantics and decided to include only those books or passages which contained references to God which were consistent with one another or which could be logically understandable or acceptable to the editors. They would have sold Judaism short and impoverished Western culture.

I. Edward Kiev

Granted that no two people sitting in the congregation have the same concept of God – how does it help the situation to drop the term? What substitutes will be used and who will decide between the valid surrogates and the invalid ones? The Freudians may object to "God the Father." The democrats to "God the King." The physicists and the astronomers may combine to eliminate the "Creator of day and night." The behaviorists might feel uncomfortable with the "still small voice." Suppose such a committee offered Tillich's "ground of being" or Kant's "ding an sich" or Bergson's "élan vital," or the Kabbalists' "en soft" or Buber's "Thou" – what greater truth or spiritual excellence would be gained thereby? It would not be long before the person lacking love in his life would be investing the "ground of being" with love and the person lacking order and purpose would be making "the thing in itself" order and purpose, and the one in a depleted and melancholy condition would be asking for the joy of life from the "élan vital."

From time to time people inquire about the oldest and most universal symbols of our faith. To the Jew, the Menorah presents a telegraphic communication of his faith. This is no time to surrender a term and its deep meaning which meant so much to endless generations of our people. What a gross irreverence to the numberless martyrs of our people who died *Al Kiddush Hashem* (even though they did not clearly define the term). It is outrageous to say: because some Jews have infantile notions of God and others illogical concepts of God, we shall drop the term from our daily worship in the home and in the synagogue. A synagogue must be a house of prayer for all people, the

Actions, Not Words

young and the old, the illiterate and the sophisticated. It is the challenge of the Rabbi and his high privilege to help his congregants to achieve ever higher and more satisfying concept of God and to develop the consensus of loyalty and acceptance which will create fellowship within and beyond the group. We do not ask a child to drop his parents when he is no longer dependent on them. He partakes of a new and more mature relationship to them. So too with God. The half-Gods and the childish Gods go to make room for the truer God, yet always retaining at least some of His earlier attributes.

Impacted in the term God are some of the richest values used which the human race has envisioned in its long march through historic time. Why should we surrender those values to those who have taken the low road, to those who have used God as the sanctioner of the baser instincts? Why should we not rather retrieve God from meaner hands and save Him to be the Guide to our nobler motives and better purposes?

I. Edward Kiev

ETHICAL FREEDOM

If we had no free will, we could not be held responsible for our actions. Repentance would be meaningless and atonement would be a mere illusion. However, since we are blessed by God with the freedom of choice, we have the capacity to turn our back on evil and sin and restore godliness to our lives.

The power to return to God is a manifestation of ethical freedom in its highest form. We believe that there is no sinner who is beyond redemption. While it is possible that the image of God within us may have been temporarily overshadowed, we have the ability to break the spell that sin has cast over us and to remove the negative and adverse emotions which have held us in bondage.

The Yom Kippur season has been set aside in Judaism for introspection and soul searching, yet we must realize that our need to return to God is a daily task and that it is an essential to normal functioning of personality as an eating, sleeping and reading. Our sages suggest that we return to God one day before we die. Since no one knows when this day will be, the need to return to God is with us at every moment of our lives. It is a perpetual and ending task. The pleading call of the prophet Hosea must forever ring in our ears: "Return O Israel, unto the Lord…"

HUMILITY, COMPASSION, ASPIRATION

There are three elements in our religious being which manifest themselves particularly on the Days of Awe. The first quality is humility, the second is compassion, and the third aspiration. True humility is the mark of the perfectly integrated personality; it combines sincere modesty about oneself, and devoted deference for God and His plan. If it derives from the concept of Teshuva – repentance or return- it is not the equivalent of servility. Repentance is a strong determination to create an understanding of the true proportion of life. It rejects all falsehood and injustice.

The second attribute, compassion, is related to the concept of Sedakah, whereby we include all of mankind in the warmth of our love and understanding. Above all it must encompass sympathy, pity, sensitivity to others, with a clear reverence for every other living thing. It is crowned by love and affection.

If humility is one's personal way of spiritual living, and compassion one's way with our neighbor, then aspiration is one's way with God.

What does God think of us? What does God want? God is waiting for us to approach him. God wants us to dedicate ourselves to His service, the service of selflessness and love and reverence. If we search for His presence, then we can meet the Divine presence.

It is for God to cause justice and righteousness to rule in the life of man: and his people Israel is to serve Him in the fulfillment of this task.

If a man performs the duty of an upright judge even for one hour, the Talmud teaches, that together

I. Edward Kiev

with God, he is the co-creator of the world. On Rosh Hashanah, which is the Day of Judgment, God the dispenser of justice, does not judge according to His own decision alone, but He causes the Host of Heaven to appear before his throne of glory and each renders his opinion.

Indeed, not only does he turn to the opinion of the angels, but he receives with due consideration the views of His people, Israel. On one occasion, when one of the Rabbis met the prophet Elijah, he asked the prophet: "What does God do?" The prophet replied: "God deliberates on the verdicts of wise men." God is therefore bound very closely with His people.

During the solemn service on Yom Kippur God even appeared in the Holy of Holies to the High Priest Ishmael and said to him: "Ishmael, my son, bless me." The priest said, "Lord of the Universe, may thy mercy overcome thine anger." And God showed that he was pleased with the benediction of Ishmael. The Talmud therefore adopts the moral: "May the blessings of an ordinary person not be unappreciated."

Actions, Not Words

FELLOWSHIP

A major tragedy of modern life lies in the fact that although people are thrown into contact with others, they feel no significant sense of true association and kinship. The links may be due to propinquity, business, coincidence. But a town does not become a community until its people share an inner togetherness and in a common life. A street does not become a neighborhood until people are united by an interrelationship of common concerns and affections. Individuals do not form a family – regardless of their legal status – until there is love, identification and sympathy. The gaps between people in our society are not being bridged by compassion, understanding and brotherliness. Living in a big city we are like individuals in a bus, finding ourselves in physical contact with one another and sharing for a time our common direction if not a common destiny, yet remaining strangers. Rabbi Akiba, the courageous and heroic teacher, said "V Chavto Lerecha Komacho" is the greatest principle in the Torah. It is certainly the greatest principle in human relations in mental health, and social progress.

We must learn to turn outer nearness into inner fellowship; the way to brotherhood is via the path that links us closer to others. The story is told that the writer Tolstoy was out on a stroll when a poor and shivering beggar asked him for help. The writer found that he left the house without any money. He said to the beggar, "I'm sorry, brother, I cannot help you." The beggar replied with deep feeling, "Thank you, kind sir, thank you very much." Tolstoy asked in astonishment, "Why do you thank me? You got nothing." "But you called me brother," replied the beggar.

Deep within each of us is a fund of brotherliness that goes unused in our bustling, corporate and competitive life. Within us too is the need to feel that another is brother to us. The relationship we crave is therefore easily attainable through our own actions and deeds.

A fence is needed, but it is not enough. We also need a bridge that links us to our fellow-men. We are not born alone, and we cannot live alone. As the anthropologist Ashley Montagu points out in his *Being Human,* mutuality and interrelatedness with our neighbors inhere in our nature and grow out of our deepest needs. To fulfill ourselves we must go forth like Joseph and say, *"Es achay onochi meyakesh,"* "I seek my brethren." William Morris said "fellowship is life and lack of fellowship is death." He was anticipated by many centuries by a sage in our Jewish tradition who exclaimed, "chevrussa o missusa," "Without companionship man perishes."

Selfhood, paradoxically enough, grows as it enters the lives of others and the life of man generally. Wholesome and sympathetic association with others is indispensable to the good and full life. Society punishes those who have offended others by committing them to enforced solitude. Hillel forecast some of the profoundest discoveries about human nature when he said, "If I am not for me, who is for me," since there is no I, no identity or individuality, what is one? The gentle teacher added, however, "and if I am for myself alone, what am I?" for he who is isolated cannot be of much worth.

I. Edward Kiev

THE ABILITY TO LISTEN

Give me an understanding heart. In the Hebrew it means a listening heart. The object being "to judge Thy people, that I may distinguish good from evil." The power to listen is the great quality of a good judge.

There are two kinds of people: Those who talk and those who listen. Solomon prayed to be among the latter category, so that he might be a true judge.

We are not judges yet, though we are always judging other people. But few of us are good listeners. Most people prefer to talk, and the less they have to say, the more they talk. Such are the foes of modesty, of peace, of truth, indeed of social life. There are, no doubt, among those who listen much and talk little, fools as well as wise men and women. But among those who talk a lot and hardly listen at all there are only fools.

This is not only bad, it is anti-religious. For the very basis of the religious spirit is the open mind, not the closed mind. The inquiring attitude, not the cocksure one. The Psalmist said "To Thee silence is praise." R. Simon ben Gamaliel said, "All my days I have grown up among the wise, and I have found nothing better than silence." The boy Samuel was taught to answer, "Speak, Lord, for Thy servant listeneth."

That is why the great scholars and teachers of humanity are the best listeners. That is why they tower above the puny, self-centered, opinionated, earthbound people who cannot listen but always talk. We cannot aspire to the dignity, the humility, and the gentle bearing of our great teachers, we can at least imitate

Actions, Not Words

their love of humanity, their concern for and interest in their neighbors, their capacity and willingness to listen. This is why Solomon had the reputation of being wise.

So should we be better men and women, and certainly better Jews, if we, too, are granted this power. Prayer for most people consists in asking God to listen to us. It would be far better if we could attune our minds to listen and hear what God has to say to us. When the Palmist said, "My soul waiteth on the Lord," he meant just this, because waiting means listening. That is the way of all revelation. That is how God reveals Himself to us even when we do not recognize the message.

I. Edward Kiev

Actions, Not Words

CHOICE, SELF-RENEWAL

I. Edward Kiev

REPENTANCE & RENEWAL

At the heart of the beautiful holiday of Rosh Hashanah is the optimism of renewal and a call to action. The holiday marks the beginning of a New Year, with its prospects of new hopes and achievements. It is called Yom Teruah, a day of new challenging trumpets.

A recurring thought in our liturgy and in the philosophical writings of the great Jewish thinkers is that God renews His world. Our rabbis declared and believed that God renews His world every day. Rosh Hashanah is the symbolic festival of such renewal and re-creation.

In the view of our faith, human life is not held helpless in the iron grip of the inevitable. All things are not pre-destined from the beginning of time. God did not create His universe and abandon it to blind necessity. God's will is continuously at work in the universe which He is forever creating, and His providence watches continuously over all His creatures. God ordained a moral order for mankind in which man shall have the chance for renewal, whenever he earnestly desires it. This is the meaning of repentance: man can wash himself clean of past sins and defilements and start fresh. There would be no meaning to morality and no point in challenging man to forsake his evil life and to adopt a new life unless such an act of regeneration were really possible.

Judaism maintains that it is possible, both for men and for nations. This is the inspiring message of the penitential season which this great Yom Hadin inaugurates. This is the optimism at the heart of our religion – a religion which is suffused with confidence in the unending rejuvenation of man and society.

God waits for man always; not only for the good man on the peaks of virtue, but also for the sinner in the lowest depths. "The gates of prayers are sometimes open and sometimes closed, but the gates of repentance are always open."

The story is told in the Midrash of a heathen woman who came to Rabbi Eliezer to be converted, saying, "Rabbi, receive me." He said to her, "Recount your acts to me." She told him of several terrible sins she had once committed. The Rabbi drove her away. She then went to Rabbi Joshua. He received her into the faith. His disciples said to him, "Rabbi Eliezer drove her away and you accept her?" He replied, "When she set her mind on becoming a Jewess, she died to her past life, and she was reborn anew."

Insofar as a man, by an act of will, reforms and remakes himself he becomes master of his spiritual destiny. His life comes into his own hands again. He is no longer sodden clay on a potter's wheel to be molded by alien hands into some involuntary design. From within and by his own will power he decisively fashions the shape and contour of his moral being. In this sense he becomes a co-creator with God, and takes on great dignity because he exercises great power, initiative and originality. Thou has made him but a little lower than the angels and has crowned him with glory and honor.

When, therefore, we wish each other on this day L'Shono Tova - "A Good Year" – we should bear in mind that the "goodness" which we pray for is largely of our own making. Whether it will be a good year in

Actions, Not Words

terms of health, prosperity and freedom from care, sorrow or suffering, is not of our own ordaining. But whether it will be a "good" year in terms of self-improvement, of intellectual and spiritual growth, of service, love, charity, and friendship, of higher virtues and deeper loyalties – that will be mainly, if not exclusively, of our own making. In the ultimate scale of values, who can say whether health and prosperity or spiritual growth is more important? Certainly, one without the other has never been known to yield life's deepest satisfactions and it's richest happiness. Both are necessary for that.

The renewal which our faith asserts is, however, not an easy-going or automatic matter. It does not come of itself, nor through mere confession of faith or formal absolution. It must be achieved through strong personal effort and spiritual exertion. There is neither physical birth nor spiritual re-birth without much travail. It is not easy to reconstruct one's life, to break acquired habits and relinquish deeply routed routines. It is not easy to cut oneself free from the tentacles of the past, from the allurements of pleasure or pleasant drifting, of material profit. But no one can be renewed without an heroic soul searching, without expiation and atonement. Man must make the effort. On this our faith is insistent. Man must make the effort because he has it in him, because God has placed within him resources sufficient to the task.

Judaism is not an easy religion. It is a summoning, demanding and challenging religion. It is a religion of *Mitzot* commandment, duties and obligations. Even if a man is not momentarily aware of any specific sin which he has committed, he is nevertheless admonished to remember that he is not perfect. "There is no man living that sinneth not." He is never absolved of the duty of deepening his life, of reaching out for new and more arduous social responsibilities. It is not peace of mind which Judaism extols as the highest good, but the service of God – which is unending and increasingly more difficult as we climb to higher levels. Our age has been too busy extolling peace of mind, yet pitiful indeed is the man whose soul is always at peace and whose heart has never known hunger or longing or sorrow. "All sunshine makes a desert," is a penetrating Oriental proverb. The truly great and good of the earth, those who wrote the immortal songs, performed the memorable deeds and carved the highways of human progress had very little peace of mind. I am inclined to be suspicious of the man who uninterruptedly enjoys undisturbed tranquility, just as I am inclined to be suspicious of the man who has never had an enemy.

The Bible nowhere calls upon men to go out in search of peace of mind. It does call upon men to go out in search of God. It calls upon men to hunger and thirst after righteousness, to seek justice and pursue it, to relieve the oppressed, to bind up the broken hearted, to proclaim liberty to the captives, and to establish peace in the world. It is an heroic enterprise in the building of the good society that our religion conceives as the destiny of man. Such an enterprise is seldom attended by ease and tranquility; frequently it is attended by persecution and suffering. "To the stars by hard ways," is the motto of one of our Western states. But these hard ways are not without their compensations. They bring with uplifting and

Actions, Not Words

sustaining interest, nourishing pride and wonderment, and, on rare occasions, even unbelievable ecstasy.

Let no man say that all such daring and doing is vain and futile. Let no one say that in this mass age, this mechanical collective civilization, the individual is less than a drone in a bee-hive, and that he cannot affect or change the vast impersonal course of human events. Let no one argue that the great days and the great opportunities are past and that all the true statesmen and leaders belonged to former generations. Do no accept that "there were giants in the land of those days," but ours is an orphaned generation, orphaned of greatness and leadership, of vision and courage.

Judaism rejects all such pessimism. It regards it as evidence of lack of faith, a form of atheism: for it omits God from its calculations - and it omits the God in man. "Be still and know that I am God! Share thy burden with the Lord and He will sustain thee." Yoke your weakness to God's all-mastering strength. "Happy is the man who strengthens himself in Thee."

God has established His world, that is shall not be moved. His eternal plans are not affected by the shifting tides in the fortunes of men and nations. The restless surface eddies of history do not deflect upon the deep channels beneath.

Men must continue to strive and aspire, to build again and yet again upon the ruins of broken hopes and shattered dreams. They must build up the old waste places, and raise up the former desolations. Men must continue to sing out, "We will not fear though the earth do change, though the mountains be hurled into the depths of the seas." We will build the city of God!

I. Edward Kiev

"God is in the midst of her, she shall not be moved. God shall help her at the approach of morning."

Rosh Hashanah reminds us not to despair of the future, nor of our own strength, nor of mankind's inexhaustible spiritual resources nor of God's cooperation. If we continue to have reverence and love for the human spirit and faith in its unfailing resurgence, we shall succeed in the end.

Actions, Not Words

PRAYER

This hour of worship is an hour wherein we try to express in prayer the very essence of our soul's yearning for God's presence, for God's sovereignty, for God's help, and for God's blessing. The act of prayer is not mere ritual contrived by some poet. It is one of those aboriginal and basic acts of the human soul, what Goethe would call *Urphanomenon,* a basic event rooted in the very character of the human spirit, a kind of archetype of the human mind. Prayer is the expression of man's needs and aspirations, addressed to the supreme source of help – to the Friend whom we recognize behind the phenomena of all existence, knowing and hoping that He is concerned about our needs and our high aspirations and through ages and ages our greatest help.

What are those needs? First and foremost health and food and life itself, without which there is nothing; then, on a higher plane, the need for forgiveness of sin and wrongdoing; and finally, the need that all the great and good causes of the human heart shall triumph, that the poor and oppressed shall be comforted, and wrongs righted, and justice done and goodness prevail.

We reverently address these prayers to a God who is moved by prayer, not just a Power but a Power who is a Shomea Tefillah – one who listens to prayers. "First Caise" (the philosopher's God) is not enough, and cosmic emotions evoked by the grandeur of nature and the universe (the poet's God) is likewise not enough. In Judaism we need a God who values what the good man values; a God who besides being the *Melech Haolam,* the "King of the Universe," is also a power "who comes to judge the earth, to judge the world with righteousness." And because God is concerned for the values which the good man values, He is open to the good man's prayers and appeal for help.

And so in the daily proper in the Amidah we always include this aspect of God" "Hear our voice, O Lord, and accept our prayer in mercy and favor, for Thou art a God who hearkenest unto prayer and supplications...Blessed art Thou O Lord who hearkenest unto prayer."

And in the same spirit our God is conceived as supporting the fallen, healing the sick, freeing the oppressed, as bringing justice to those who are robbed, as giving bread to the hungry, as opening the eye of the blind, as loving the righteous.

These are the demands of the human heart, and sometimes the response seems to many of us not fully adequate. But, mark you, despite repeated and recurrent and constant failure to receive instant response to those cries for help, man is so convinced of their utter rightness, of the power of these claims he makes upon the world and therefore to God, that he will not take no for an answer. No failure can discourage or refute him. So it must be recognized that prayer issues from the depths which our philosophy dreams not of, and cannot plumb, and therefore cannot invalidate. The things man prays for, his life, his ideals of justice and goodness, are felt to be so supremely important that the very stars in their courses are expected to fight for their realization and preservation.

What of the prayers that we think are not answered? Such a failure does not wither the urge to

Actions, Not Words

pray, nor dry up the deep source or wellspring from which prayers naturally surge up. Do we recognize the viewpoint often expressed by scientists that the universe is a system of rigid necessity, that the world cannot be cajoled or changed; that things have to be as they are; and that it is therefore a childish fantasy to think we can budge or refashion them?

The Jewish and the religious viewpoint holds that the world is not fixed for all eternity but has an open future which we can help make or mar, above all that the universe is proceeding with a purpose and towards a goal – no matter how falteringly or dimly – which it is our task to help achieve: that it is not devoid of direction, or of concern for values that men cherish – justice, goodness, love – but on the contrary, finds its whole meaning and original intention in the emergence and flowering of those ultimate ends.

This belief is the deepest intuition of the best of the race at all times and among all peoples: an intuition, an anticipation, an act of faith: the faith that what our heart wants, the universe also wants and God wants.

If it is not true, maybe it is not yet true but will be. Maybe it is our task as human beings to be helpers and co-creators with our God who is still in the process of total realization, who needs our strength to carry out His designs as we need His strength to hearten us. Maybe God and perfection are at the end and not at the beginning. Maybe perfection is to be achieved, and not something to start with.

Our own prophets and our prayer book seem to have had an inkling of this. At culminating points in our service we say in a phrase, On that Day He shall be One and His name shall be One. On that day, not as yet

I. Edward Kiev

alas, but surely on that day He shall be One, as He is not yet one in the hearts of all men.

Prayer, one often feels, is a forgotten art today even among those who still consider themselves deeply religious and who pray regularly every day. Possibly there were never many who could *really* pray; perhaps we have deluded ourselves in believing that in other times the art of devotion was more widespread than it is now. Men with the gift of prayer have always been emotional; for plain people, praying may always have been more a matter of routine than of necessity. We find an instructive admonition in the Mishna, "Do not practice set prayer." In other words, avoid making your prayer commonplace and mechanical. One of our early rabbis would have exempted from prayer any Jew "who found praying burdensome," who prayed only as a kind of dull duty, a conventional act to be gotten over with quickly. Another rabbi would invalidate the prayer of anyone who could not create some new aspect in it, probably not meaning new words and sentences, but the capacity to continually bring a fresh comprehension and sensitivity to the same ancient, well-known text. Thus, even some of Judaism's early teachers were already shocked by the lackluster prayer formulas, and instead sought men for whom every act of prayer was a new, unique experience.

The power of prayer is not, indeed, unlimited, nor is it always possible to strike every moment when God is "accessible" and lets Himself be swayed, yet if a man's prayer is genuine and offered in sincerity, it does have an effect – first of all upon himself.

Man cannot alter the cosmic order by prayer, he cannot break through the chain of law and necessity that binds natural events and brings about a miracle, but he can integrate or re-integrate himself in the general scheme of existence and events and thus obtain succor for his need. If a man's two legs have been amputated he knows quite well that no matter how much he might pray, new legs will not grow. But prayer may give him the strength to live in harmony (or greater harmony) with himself and the world without legs. Through prayer he has the power to de-egocentrize himself, and achieve a state of reconciliation with his fate. Through prayer he may sometimes discover in himself such hidden or dormant sources of delight in and gratitude for his very existence as will greatly compensate him for his loss.

One of the aspects of prayer, undoubtedly, is just this turning to oneself, this navigation of the depths of one's own so largely unknown soul, this discovery of strata of our own being in which there is hardly any contact in daily, diffuse living.

I. Edward Kiev

Actions, Not Words

LIVING THE PRESENT

I. Edward Kiev

SIMPLE PLEASURES

Oliver Wendell Holmes once said, "If you haven't cut your name on the door by the time you've reached forty, you might just as well put up your jack-knife." But Holmes himself wrote some of his best works when he was in his seventies. Goethe completed *Faust* at eighty. Titian painted his historic masterpiece of the Battle of Lepanto at ninety-eight. Henrietta Szold's Hadassah work didn't begin until she was in her late sixties. Chaim Weizmann became the first president of Israel in his middle seventies. Ben Gurion in his eighties founded the college in the Negev at Sedeh Boker. Golda Meir, in her seventies, was called out of retirement to again head her country.

Yet despite the blessings of old age, often still strong productive energies, and the fact that we all aspire to it, in old age we suffer from too many physical limitations for them to constitute the best years of our lives. Perhaps the most obvious burden is reflected in the passage of the *Shma Kolenu* prayer: "Cast us not off in old age; when our strength departs, forsake us not." The haunting dread of being cast off, of loneliness and of being forsaken, these are the overwhelming fears of old age which too often rob it of the peace and serenity it could and should offer, and rule it out as the best times of our lives.

What, then, are the best years of our lives? The answer is that the best years of our lives are to be found in the present – right now. This year can be the best year of our life, for this is the only year we have at our disposal.

I. Edward Kiev

Unlike the modern writer who declared "Youth is a blunder, manhood a struggle, old age a regret," we must discover our blessings in each of life's stages understand the responsibilities and fulfill them.

As Ralph Waldo Emerson said, "This time, like all times, is a very good one, if we but know what to do with it." The present is life's holy ground. It is the hallowed meeting place of two eternities – the past and the future. If we try to live in either of those, however, we are courting emotional and physical disaster. And to our everlasting loss, we are missing the abundant satisfactions so close to hand. It is in the present alone that we can and must live, in each "unforgiving minute" which comes laden with blessings beyond number.

It doesn't really take something exciting or spectacular or sensational to make this the best year of our lives. The exciting and the spectacular only delight momentarily and leave us later more painfully aware of life's humdrum existence. Daily happiness comes from quiet, simple, unspectacular satisfactions: pleasant hours with our family, moments lived in the presence of great spirits whose books we read or whose music we listen to, a bit of study, working for a communal cause, a few minutes of daily prayer. These are not by any means spectacular, but these are the things that really make life meaningful and satisfying.

"Life," Woodrow Wilson correctly observed, "is not all running to a fire." Helen Keller, when asked what she would most want to see if she could have her eyesight restored for a moment, answered, "The smile on a child's face and a sunset."

Actions, Not Words

Our saints and teachers taught us life yet spurned their years. For them life was piety and righteousness, the holiness conferred on little things. "To love the Lord thy God," they said, "that is life and the length of thy days." Their percept and example persuade us that righteousness, even in their death, may be called "living."

Let there be life for us; to find the holiness in little things, to see our brief moment as part of God's eternity, to love with all our hearts, not the pettiness that fills our days, but the beauty and goodness and truth that move our souls.

I. Edward Kiev

ACCEPT THE UNIVERSE

Ours is a time of deep darkness, yet it offers a dazzling dawn. It is a time of hope-shattering fear, yet it lends itself to soul-building faith. It is a time of doubt and despair, and yet it is still bliss to be alive – bliss for any and all of us – even the oldest and the unhappiest, even those who are convinced that there is nothing left for which to live. It is a time that seems tragic for youth, but to be young today can be "very heavenly." It is a great time to be alive.

The end of the word has been predicted since the world began, yet there is no evidence of even the beginning of the end. Our world had died a thousand deaths, but it still lives. Edgar Rice Burroughs, the renowned naturalist, once cried: "A better world I have never wanted. I could not begin to exhaust the knowledge and the delights of this one. I have found in it deep beneath deep, worlds within a world – the endless series of beautiful and wonderful forms forever flowing out of itself. From the highest heavens of the telescope to the minutest organisms of the microscope, all is beautiful and wonderful and passeth all understanding."

It has been said that an optimist believes that ours is the best of all possible worlds; a pessimist is afraid that it really is. A half-filled glass of water may be seen as half-full or half-empty, depending on whether one's mental spectacles are optimist-tinted or pessimist-colored. Too many of us see the world as all good or all bad. Neither, of course, is accurate.

Life, like the glass, is at the same time both filled and empty – filled with an abundance of achievement, devoid of sufficient fulfillment. There is, however, a third way of looking at it: through the bifocals of a Wordsworth, for example, who would give the empty space in the glass only a fleeting glance, then proceed to rejoice in the remaining life – refreshing water. Wise old Job was using bifocals when, at the close of his bitter tirade against the cruel evils and ills that man encounters in God's world, he confessed: "I know that Thou canst do everything; and that no purpose can be withholden from Thee. Who is this that hideth counsel without knowledge? Therefore, have I uttered that which I understand not; things too wonderful for me, which I knew not."

The eyeglasses of our faith – not blind faith- are always bifocal. Below is the lens that provides the nearsighted view, bringing into bold relief all the objectionable features of human living. As the eye lifts to look through the upper lens, designed to correct the astigmatic sight, it sees life in larger, wider, deeper perspective. It sees it "steadily and whole." It beholds the background of good as well as the foreground evil; the hills of joy as well as the valley of sorrow. And it sends back a message to the soul of man affirming that, despite denial and defeat, disease and death, and perhaps even because of its tears and fears, the world is a wonderful place.

We're all equipped with the bifocals of faith. Most of us, however, use only the lower lens. Even as the physical eye finds it easier to look down than up, and at that which is widely spaced – so do our mental eyes develop the tendency to cultivate the downward look and limited observation.

I. Edward Kiev

The teachers in the Talmud hotly debated the question whether it was better that man had been born or whether it would have been better if he had never been born at all. They finally decided it would have been much better, for man as well as for the world, if he had never been born. But since he had been thrust into life, they added, it was his duty to aspire nobly and build gloriously. Margaret Fuller, the New England pioneer of Unitarianism, resigned herself to the reality of existence when she said: "I accept the universe." The caustic comment of the curmudgeon, Thomas Carlyle, was "By gad, she'd better."

Sooner or later the mature among us learn to accept this universe just as it is – gratefully, not grudgingly, because it is the only one we have. It is the infantile among us who continue to complain petulantly that the world owes them life as well as a living. One of Buddha's parables tells of a Hindu mother who was overjoyed when she finally gave birth to a son. Just when the boy was able to walk, he died. The young mother carried the dead child clasped to her breast, running through the village from house to house, pleading for some medicine that might restore her son to life. Most of the people looked upon her as mad and sadly shook their heads. Finally she came upon a wise old man and she prayed: "Lord and master, do you know of any medicine that will give my son back to me?" "I know of only one – a handful of mustard seed taken from a house where no son, no husband, no parent, and no servant has ever died."

Clearly, it serves no useful purpose to ask the impossible. The world owes us nothing, not even life. *We owe the world everything.* It was chance, not

Actions, Not Words

certainty, that gave us birth. A kind providence reached into the heart of eternal darkness and brought us forth into the blessing of the light of life. Death is the price paid for the privilege of life. Just a tap on the shoulder by our Father in Heaven to remind us that our part in the drama of mankind has been played, and that we now must make some room for other players and go back to the same hidden unknown from which we came. Even a slight stay on earth, lasting just a day, is a gift from God.

In "The Story of San Michele," Axel Munthe reminds us: "All that is really beautiful is not put up for sale at all, but is offered us as gifts by the immortal god. We are allowed to watch the sun rise and set, the clouds sailing around in the sky, the forests and fields, the glorious sea, all without spending a penny. The birds sing to us for nothing; the wild flowers we may pick as we are walking along the roadside. There is no entrance fee to the starlit hall of the night...A few friends, a few books, indeed a very few, and a dog is all you need to have about you as long as you have yourself."

There are gifts which man would reject if he could, such as sorrow and old age and death. But Montaigne makes a very helpful observation when he says: "Should a man fall into the aches and impotencies of age from a sprightly and vigorous youth, on the sudden, I do not think humanity capable of enduring such a change. But nature, leading us by the hand in an easy, as it were, an insensible pace, little by little, step by step, conducts us gently to that miserable condition and by that means makes it familiar to us so that we perceive not, or are sensible of the stroke then, when

I. Edward Kiev

our youth dies in us, though it be really a harder death than the final dissolution of a languishing body, which is only the death of old age."

But even these changes in our bodies and minds are not without their compensations. The melting tears of the snows of sorrow can enrich the soul of the human spirit and prepare it for a harvest of noble character and rare wisdom. The yellowed parchment face of old age is a palimpsest that has buried under its wrinkled surface solid layers of remembered experience and ripened understanding, capable of providing treasured hours of comfort and contentment. Even the imperious, inexorable summons of death is often a welcome writ of release from long servitude to years of pain and shame, defeat and despair, frustration and fear.

Sooner or later the mature among us learn to accept the world in which we live. Only the callow keep up the moon baying process of wishing they had been born in a different generation, or keep striving to prolong their youth into advanced age. Nothing is more pathetic than the sight of an aging man playing the Don Juan games of adolescence or of an overly-made-up old lady behaving like a flirtatious coquette. Nothing is more vain than for the children of our atomic age to sigh away their days yearning for the legendary bliss of a pre-atomic world. We must come to terms with the universe in our age and period of history.

Every time is a good time in which to be alive. Ours is the responsibility to make it good for us. "The world is too big and too fast. There is too much doing – too many wards, crimes, casualties, excitement and marvels – try as you will, you get behind in the race in

Actions, Not Words

spite of yourself. It is an incessant strain to keep pace, and still you lose ground. Science empties its discoveries upon you so fast that you stagger beneath them in hopeless bewilderment; the political world gets up new scenes so fast that you are out of breath trying to keep up with them – so many shouting at the world with all their might to get the world's attention that your head whirls like a whirl-top. Everything is high pressure. Human nature cannot endure so much." This was written in 1837 and appeared in the *Atlantic Journal* in connection with the inauguration of the transatlantic cable.

Every man in every age can find his world good - but he himself must make it so. His golden age can be the present of reality instead of the past of his imagination. The same world can be good for my neighbor, but bad for me. The world itself is neutral and impersonal in its relation to man. It offers all it has and asks for nothing in return. It is orderly, dependable and cooperative. It is for man to use it wisely, not foolishly; to plant the seeds of love, not hate; to reap a harvest of joy, not sorrow. "Here we are," cries George Meredith, "you and I, and the millions of men and animals about us: the innumerable atoms which make up our bodies, blown as it were by mysterious processes together, so that there has happened, just now, for every one of us, the wonder of wonders, we have come to life. And here we stand, with our senses, our keen intellects, our infinite desires, our nerves quivering to the touch of joy or pain: beacons of brief fire, burning between two unexplored extremities. What are we to make of this wonder while it is still ours?"

I. Edward Kiev

We can – if we use our bifocals of faith – look at the world through the upper lens and with complete confidence exclaim: "Behold it is good." Most of it has truly been put into the dominion of our hands and under the control of our feet. We have been made partners with God in much of the work of creation. We are in large measure masters of our fate and captains of our soul. So much of what we have found bad in nature or human nature we have conquered and controlled and even converted into good.

Our world is haunted by the growing fear that man will not survive simply because the earth will not be able to nourish and support him. These calamity-criers present the thesis that man faces the danger of possible physical extinction because of his careless handling of the food resources of the earth's soil. The human race has increased more rapidly than its capacity to provide sufficient nutrition. They forget that man's ingenuity has never yet failed to meet extreme challenges. If the coal supply threatens to be exhausted, there is hydro-electric power. If electricity fails to keep pace with our "souped –up" civilization, there is the split atom. So, too, if the soil cannot satisfy the hunger needs of the human body, there are within reach the unplumbed, vitamin-filled chemical substances of the sea and sky. Whenever a flood or famine has swept over man, a Noah's ark of salvation has always been fashioned to float him to survival. It will continue in the present and future as it has in the past.

In the face of the swiftly advancing hosts of the miracles of medicine, disease is beating a stubborn, but steady retreat. Man is gradually developing mastery over the ills of the mind as well as his body. He is

Actions, Not Words

lengthening his years on earth, lessening his fears of heaven. He is reducing his menacing hazards of hatred and the dangerous consequences of crime. He is eliminating the evil and enthroning the good.

On a more personal level, you and I are freer today than man has ever been; we live longer and our work is easier; we own more, have more leisure and far more security; we are not oppressed by a multitude of terrorizing superstitions; our education is fuller, and our visions of a better world wider and higher.

We must think of what we have *today* – not what we had yesterday, not what we may have tomorrow. When I was young a wise person told me the story of an Indian princess who was given a basket and told that she might pick the finest ears of corn she could find in a certain prized field. There was but one condition: She had to choose as she went along. She could never retrace her steps, never go back even so far as her hand might reach.

Admiring the fine ears of corn that met her gaze, the princess carefully felt one ear after another. But she left them on the stalks as she moved on, thinking always of the better ears that might lie ahead. And so she went until she had passed the last stalk of the last row – basket empty, wishes and hopes not once fulfilled.

I tell that story so that we may realize how much of today's joy we can miss if we are always longing for yesterday or preparing to enjoy ourselves "tomorrow," instead of accepting and cherishing the present.

Well have our Rabbis taught us to bless the Lord for the evil as well as the good that may confront us. For both are very relative terms. We can never

I. Edward Kiev

appreciate the good unless we have been forced, alas, to partake of evil. Very often, as we drink from the Cup of Sorrow, we learn to appreciate more fully the good which we had always taken for granted. Each day confronts us with many challenges. We must learn to face them and to capitalize on them. No matter how great the suffering and painful the sorrow, whatever else we lose, we must never lose hope.

Thus as we stand at the threshold of the year 5715, let us resolve to make the best of each day. Day by day let no hour pass without our having helped the poor, alleviated the suffering and pain of the sick, comforted the bereaved, and helped all who turn to us for guidance. Leading that kind of life we will never be driven to morbidity by the thought that the Clock of Time is ticking so fast, and before we know it has passed by us so quickly.

Actions, Not Words

LET US BEGIN

None of us can see beyond the horizon of our own times. What lies ahead no one knows. But Judaism reminds us that beyond all horizons, there is God. Always God will be there and mankind will be there; God's unfolding purpose which embraces all in its eternal processes, and our own brief and passing generations will be there and will prevail.

Our teachers and sages cautioned us not to deprecate our own times nor our own leaders. Commenting on the verse in Koheleth, "One generation goes and another generation comes." The Rabbis declared, "Your own generation should be regarded by you as great as any past generation." And there is another verse in Koheleth which reads: "Say not thou: How was it that the former days were better than these, for it is not out of wisdom that thou speakest thus."

Each age has its records of triumphs and failures. In every age men have been inclined to extol the past, deprecate the present, and be apprehensive of the future. No age is idyllic. Each age has its leaders. No leader quite matches his hour. But each age adds something to human progress, and so does every true leader of men.

We must never forget that regardless of how vast our world is, how rigidly organized, and how ruthlessly coordinated, the individual man and woman is still its moral nucleus. In the long run society will reflect the fundamental moral aspirations of the individual men and women who compose it: that is to say, of those men and women who are determined enough and willing enough to make their moral ideals come true regardless of the cost to themselves. This nuclear moral theory, when it is released by the individual can disrupt all the seemingly unshakable worlds of indurate tyranny and injustice. There is always room for the pioneer. There is always need for the dreamer of great dreams.

On the surface it looks as though our times are not sensitive enough for moral optimism or idealism. There is a real danger of a defeatist mood sweeping over our people, especially our young people – the mood of "Oh, what's the use?"

What hopeless, disastrous confusion exists in so many places in our land!

It will hearten us to observe that the imperative Herculean labors of mankind are nevertheless going on in spite of confusion and strife. Many of the oppressed peoples of the earth who have long been denied their freedom have recently achieved or are in the process of achieving their freedom and independence. They are on the road to a new and better life. Knowledge is increasing and so is the health of people everywhere. Long and hard is the road of a better social order and a world at peace, and among many of the pitfalls, there is a road, there is a goal, and we have learned to follow it unwearied.

We cannot always wait to do the thing which needs to be done until we see the road clearly ahead. Sometimes we must act in faith and courage, even when we do not know what lies ahead. Sometimes we must move forward through mist and fog. "If we would know where we are," declared Abraham Lincoln, "and whither we are tending, we could better judge what to do and how to do it." And yet, Lincoln was not deterred from action by the manifold bewilderments which beset him. He did what had to be done with the material and opportunities which lay at hand, trusting that what he honestly was striving to do would be within the true and abiding design of human progress.

"Thine is not the duty to complete the task," declared our sages, "but neither art thou free to desist from it."

I. Edward Kiev

Actions, Not Words

JEWISH SURVIVAL

I. Edward Kiev

OUR 300-YEAR HISTORY

Stop to think, if you will, what would have been the fate of world Jewry had America not been open to us 300 years ago, and had Jews not made the mark they did in every area of American life- in science, in government, in social service, in business, in philanthropy. I do not think it would be an exaggeration to say that the fate of European Jewry, as a result of the last holocaust, would have been even more disastrous than it was. Not six million would have been lost, but perhaps eight or even ten million might have been exterminated. There would not have been a State of Israel. The remnants that were saved in Africa and Yemen and a host of other countries would long have languished and perished through disease and persecution.

In all these far flung areas of the world the influence of American Jewry looms great and it is well for us to consider on this tercentenary the beginning and growth of American Jewry – the struggles and problems of our forbearers and, particularly, to try to arrive at an understanding of the inner strength of our ancestors who made it all possible.

Despite the wide influence of American Jewry, the history of the Jew in America is very short and limited in relation to the history of our civilization as a whole, which is many thousands of years old.

Our function today, rather than trying to review the history of three centuries of Jews in America, is to *understand* the history of the Jews in our glorious land.

Goethe once that that "That which history can give us best is the *enthusiasm* which it raises in our hearts."

I. Edward Kiev

Let us see what we can learn from the experiences of our immediate ancestors that will make us understand them better and inspire us to carry on in their noble tradition.

The story of the Jew in America is the story of the Jew who wouldn't say "die" – it is the story of the Jew who knew the difference between right and wrong and always fought for what was right and decent and democratic. And that fight goes back to the very first day that Jews set foot on the shores of New Amsterdam on September 22, 1654.

From that day, when a boatload of twenty-three Jews arrived on this continent from Brazil, they were met by a spirit of hostility by the head of the Dutch Colony. Despite the fact that New Amsterdam, as New York was then called, had a population of less than one thousand people speaking eighteen different languages, Peter Stuyvesant was so bigoted and narrow that he couldn't bear the presence of this new group which, after all, could not have affected the nature of the colony which was already far from homogeneous in background and outlook.

And so the interminable fight began. The fight for acceptance, for equality, for human rights. If ever Macaulay's analysis was right, it was right in the light of Jewish history. "A man is not worth his salt," said Macaulay, "in whose belly a fire is not burning." A fire was burning in the belly of the Jews from the moment they arrived in New Amsterdam when they heard that the attitude of Peter Stuyvesant was similar. They would not be bulled. They remembered their Bible, and how God said to Moses who complained that the Jews were trapped between the Egyptians and the Sea:

Actions, Not Words

"Tell the children of Israel to move on. There is no going backward!" And the Jews of Amsterdam, many of whom were stockholders in the West Indies Co., let their voices be heard: The Jews must be permitted to stay in New Amsterdam, they cannot go back to Spain or Portugal because of the Inquisition; moreover they had "risked their possessions and their blood" to defend Dutch interests in Brazil.

Nevertheless it was a continuous, unrelenting fight that had to be waged. A fight to own property, to own a house, to operate a business, a fight to even be allowed to accept equal responsibilities in the military service. Jews were *denied* the right to "stand guard" and because they did not serve, a special tax was imposed upon them. But men like Asser Levy and Jacob Barsimson were unwilling to accept such ridiculous conditions, made a fight for equal rights, and they won.

If there is any one characteristic that marks American Jewish history, it is this burning passion not to be taken advantage of, not to be a second class citizen, not to be bullied by despots or by their undemocratic rule.

In 1685 it was the fight for the right to conduct public worship. The law on the books granted protection only to those "Who professed faith in God by Jesus Christ."

It took one hundred years before Jews enjoyed full naturalization rights. It was in 1740 that the battle was won to omit the words "Upon the true faith of a Christian," from the oath of naturalization.

The battle for equal rights and the freedom to pursue one's own religious beliefs was a never-ending

I. Edward Kiev

one. From the beginning, Jews have fought for the separation of church and state. In Pennsylvania in 1784 a fight took shape over the rights of Jews to become members of the General Assembly without subscribing to a belief in the divine inspiration of both the Old and the New Testaments.

In 1861 it was the battle over the rights of Jews to have a Chaplain in the armed forces of the Union Army. But before this could be done the law had to be changed and the words stating that a "Chaplain must be a regularly ordained minister of some Christian denomination," had to be deleted from the statute books. Congress paid little heed to complaints of inequality and it was only after sufficient pressure was exerted, that President Lincoln agreed to advocate the change in the law. General Grant issued order No. 11 against the Jewish tradesmen.

All these are mere samplings from American Jewish history which could be multiplied many fold. Suffice it to note that they all point to one great characteristic of the Jew that came to the fore in every crisis: whenever the problem was great, whenever the barrier seemed impassable, they moved ahead – continued to fight for what was good and just.

But there is still another element we could not overlook in evaluating the under-currents of American Jewish history – namely, the existence of a certain intangible sensitivity that has become part of the very fiber and being of every Jew.

A profound sensitivity which motivated the Jew to have an understanding of the true values of life, to the ideals of equality, democracy and freedom which he felt were basic to good living for himself and for the

Actions, Not Words

world. Through the lifeline of his history there has come down to each Jew an uncanny sense of consciousness of people and events. The act itself was never as important as the purpose behind it.

What was Asser Levy fighting for when he wanted to serve as guard? Was he so anxious to be a soldier? Or in the fight for a Jewish chaplain, when the military installations containing Jews were limited? They were fighting against the *intent* of the laws.

This keen perception which has enabled the Jews to understand the significance of isolated events has been their saving grace. If Jews have met with success in America, it is only because they were able to couple this keen faculty of understanding the intent of a law with moving on and taking action.

This is the story behind the history of the Jews in America. It has been an exciting and eventful history, but even more it has been a purposeful one. The many feats of heroism and sacrifice that Jews have displayed through the lives of men like Asser Levy, Hay Salomon, Judah Touro, Judah P. Benjamin, the Franks family, the Lehmans, Justice Brandeis and Justice Cardozo, have all helped make America safe and great not only for Jews, but for all its citizens.

I. Edward Kiev

RELIGIOUS FREEDOM

This is a time for spiritual stock taking, for a *Cheshbon Hanefesh*. We look back on the road we have traveled, we examine the stage we have reached, we strive to look ahead on the road before us insofar as it is given man's vision to penetrate the endless vistas.

Let us for the sake of perspective realize that grand anniversaries are not rare events for the Jewish people. How could they be with 4,000 years of history behind us? Let us only mention the 800th anniversary of Maimonides, the great sage and master of the Middle Ages, the 3,000th anniversary of the founding of Jerusalem.

But this anniversary is of commanding importance to us Jews in America as well as to our Christian brothers.

From its very beginning this great broad land of ours has been a magnet for many worthy ambitions, the lode-star of many hopes and aspirations, but among these ambitions, hopes and aspirations, none has been more powerful and enduring than the longing to escape from persecution, the yearning "to breathe free," as Emma Lazarus expressed it in her famous sonnet.

This longing for freedom, primarily religious freedom, has impelled men and women of many origins and creeds to the shores of America. In 1620 it brought the Mayflower with its hundred passengers to the rock-bound coast of New England, those we call the Pilgrim Fathers. In a real sense, a spiritual sense, they are the fathers of all Americans, irrespective of origin or faith, who cherish the ideals of freedom.

Actions, Not Words

In 1654, the same longing brought the first Jewish passengers, on the St. Charles, to the shores of New Amsterdam; in the decades and centuries that followed, men and women of other faiths and from all lands of the Old World streamed to America. But in the case of no other people has this urge to escape from persecution been so potent and continuous as in the case of Jews, for no other people has been the victim of a siege of persecution so long and so cruel.

So that immigration wave of 1654 - if one can call so small a ripple a wave – was followed by more and larger waves, among them the "forty-eighters" who fled from German and Austria, and the great wave from Russia and Poland which began in 1881. And after 300 years, and primarily since that year when the great influx from Eastern Europe began, we have grown to an aggregate of over five million people, the largest community in the entire history of the Jews.

But numbers alone are not important. We are not only a large, but a free community, free individually and collectively. We are free under the wings of the American eagle, free because America as a whole is free, free with a freedom we would forfeit, if, God forbid, America as a whole lost its freedom. And we are also a prosperous community which, like our freedom, is part and parcel of the prosperity of America. And this freedom and prosperity make it possible for us to bring into play whatever gifts the Creator bestowed on us, with the result that we are not only free and prosperous, but also an influential community.

So as we look back on the three-hundred-year road we have traveled, we have a right to feel humbly proud

I. Edward Kiev

and deeply grateful – grateful to the God of our fathers who provided this safe and bountiful haven in our difficult journey, and grateful to this might land of freedom and opportunity.

We have marched forward on this road together with America as a whole. We have marched with her bold pioneers across the continent toward her vanishing frontiers. We have toiled and struggled and suffered together with them. We have marched with America, onward toward the expanding boundaries of her industries and commerce, her science and invention, her literature, her music, her drama, her art. We have sat in the councils of her statesmen, we have fought and bled and died on her battlefields. Do we owe a debt to America? Indeed we do. It is the same dept owed by all others who live under her sheltering wings. It is a continuous debt that is never liquidated. We have paid it and shall continue to pay it gladly and proudly.

But we have another debt, a debt to ourselves as a community and a debt to our people – wherever they dwell. Is there a conflict between our obligations to America and our obligations to ourselves and our people? Does America demand of us that we erase our momentous past, denounce our historic kinship, deny our inner selves?

To ask that question is to answer it with a thunderous *no*. Such a demand would itself be a conflict with America, in conflict with her noblest traditions, her great ideals and standards of freedom.

Our obligation to ourselves as a community – a Jewish community – requires us, first and foremost, to insure the continuity of our heritage of faith and traditions by transmitting them to our children.

I. Edward Kiev

MAINTAINING OUR JUDAISM

It is so easy to get lost in the world. And because it is, we come to the synagogue to find ourselves. And if we are to find ourselves, we must look at that which is greater than ourselves, toward God Himself. This is the true significance of our prayer.

We find ourselves when we discover that we are children of God, who have been given life as a trust, to be lived in a way worthy of Him who trusted it to our care. On the day of Yom Kippur we submit all our errors and sins to be judged by God and seek His forgiveness.

If we American Jews are not to get lost in the world, we will have to take our Judaism seriously. Casual Jews too often become Jewish casualties. Taking Judaism seriously involves more than financial responsibility to the synagogue or to the UJA or to similar important causes. It is not only a question of giving. It is also a matter of taking, taking what is rightly ours, what a hundred generations of Jews have accumulated for us to enjoy.

It means enjoying the liberation from enslavement to work by enjoying our Sabbath and our festivals and religious endeavors.

Earnest observers are questioning our future as Jews because they see beneath the surface a dilution of the contents of Jewish life, a slow but steady process of attrition eating away at the vitals of Jewish life; hallowed observances being discarded; Jewish homes emptied of any distinctive Jewish content, or symbols and sounds or rituals; Jewish lives losing all uniqueness.

Actions, Not Words

Because the process is gradual and largely voluntary because the inner corrosion is taking place under the cover of feverish outward activity, we are prone to develop a false sense of security. The sober truth is that for the American Jew it is very easy to get lost in the world.

The problems of getting lost is one which not only confronts us as Americans, and as Jews, but also as human beings. Life, like a careless laundryman, has a nasty way of shrinking our ideals and our hopes, bleaching the color out of our values and our principles. We come into maturity carrying the banner of youthful enthusiasm and noble goals only to suffer what the poet Shelley called "the contagion of the world's slow stain."

There is no simple or single explanation why we get lost in the world. The more persuasive reasons seem to include the addiction to and worship of success, the insatiable hunger for these things, the soul-consuming preoccupation with status. These things combine to blur our vision. They throw our sense of values out of focus so we blink at the truth of an old proverb which teaches that he who sacrifices his conscience to ambition burns the picture to obtain the ashes. They cause us to confuse a man's worth with his wealth, his stature with his status. We forget that what a man is, is of infinitely more significance than what a man has. We have come as human beings who are so easily diverted from the highroad of life into its alleys and byways.

Temptation, false values, loss of confidence, lack of courage – these are only some of the pitfalls. Pettiness, selfishness, fear are others.

I. Edward Kiev

No one has the right to say to another fellow adventurer: Friend, you have lost the way. But each of us has an obligation to ask ourselves- *Have I lost the way?* Have I turned my back on what I know to be true and just? Have I betrayed my own finest instincts? Have I misused God's gift of body and mind?

Yom Kippur is the ultimate spiritual experience in which we seek atonement. It is a time which summons us to make repairs, to retrace the steps that have gone astray, to undo – while time remains and opportunity permits – the wrongs we are doing to ourselves and others.

Above all, the day of Yom Kippur whispers to each of us with divine insistence: Your primary duty is to find yourself, and not to get lost in the world!

Actions, Not Words

YOM KIPPUR

Yom Kippur, moving and unique in a hundred ways, reassesses for us our place in the world as Jews and as men and women. At this season, every Jew feels himself one of the House of Israel in its historic onward march. None so witless or weary as to fail to sense a renewal of Jewish consciousness and Jewish loyalty, a deeper realization of the Jewish heritage, a higher appreciation of our Jewish destiny. Every one of us knows also that in the traditional rites and ceremonies on this day we stand before the Lord of the Universe as responsible human beings to be judged by our thoughts and actions in relation to Heaven and to all the world. Nowhere can be found a court where special interests are excluded as they are on this judgment day. The immortal soul of each Jew – as Jew and person – seeks union with the Universal Spirit.

I. Edward Kiev

A TIME FOR VALUES

The commandment and its message are as clear and valid today as on the day Moses spoke to the children of Israel. "See I set before you this day life and prosperity, death and adversity. Chose life – if you and your offspring would live."

These are times when we must hold fast to the great values transcending the physical and the temporal. What values shall we choose – those of today or tomorrow, or of a future that is close at hand? This is not time for asceticism or escapism. The values of today are good, and those of tomorrow are good and those of a future that is not remote. All are entwined in the pattern wherein the ideal of life and its values form the very essence of our liturgy at this High Holy Day season. The emphasis is made repeatedly as we rise to invoke God's blessing during each Amidah beginning with our prayers on Rosh Hashanah and concluding with the NEILAH prayer as the sun sets on Yom Kippur.

One thing is clear that whatever values we choose for ourselves, we rediscover at this season the highest value for today is the sanctity of life, the sanctity of our being, the sanctity of all life under God's heaven. The pursuit of this ideal is the greatest and noblest purpose to which the Jewish people dedicates itself at this season.

Actions, Not Words

ROSH HASHANAH

There are two basic views of the importance of this great day. One, very ancient, holds that the universe took form on this day. (Rosh Hashanah, Hayom Haras Olam.) The second view is concerned with the ethical and philosophical concept whereby judgment is rendered on high all over creation. Within these ideas we find the traditional basis of a God-centered world, wherein for ages our people has recognized the Divine source of all creation and the sovereignty of the God of Israel as the supreme ruler and judge of all mankind.

The historic lesson of our people has given Rosh Hashanah another dimension. While we commemorate the creation and Divine judgment we are also made aware of the place Israel has played in universal life and universal affairs. Thus through the ages this great festival is also cited as the *Yom Hazikkaron*, the Day of Memorial. In this connection the memorial, this *Zikkaron,* has greater significance than the term which we customarily use for special prayers for the departed or for generations who have perished. This memorial is true recall of the living creative forces which have shaped our people's life and thought, our courage and strength, our struggle with the forces of darkness and evil and our triumphant challenge to proclaim freedom and peace as the most important goals of mankind. Only with their attainment will the ultimate liberation of humanity from the terrors of war and self-destruction be realized, and the recognition come that above all law and power there is one supreme Divine law which can inspire love and respect and brotherhood in the hearts of humanity.

I. Edward Kiev

So we see that Rosh Hashanah serves several purposes. It reminds of us God's greatness and goodness (*Hamechadesh bechol Yom Betuvo Maase Bershit*). We become aware of our own frailty and insecurity (*Me Onu Me Chayenu*). So our faith in a merciful and just God instills within us a sense of *Bittachon* in the face of the greatest disturbances and loss of tranquility. The divine *Hashgocho*, the Divine providence, we believe watches over us to guide us and help us through the most difficult times.

Again this is a time of Jewish self-identification, an opportunity to say and feel that we are Jews. It is a time for renewing and strengthening family ties, and for remembering and greeting friends.

But above all else this is a truly religious holiday, an affirmation of the cosmic Divine concern for man, a declaration that God cares about our destiny and our deeds.

Actions, Not Words

HANUKKAH

As we kindle this first Hanukkah light and begin our eight-day celebration, we must pause and watch this taper and think about all things it symbolizes and what it means to us. We think about our own commitment to our faith.

Does your commitment have the life span of this candle, or does it have the life span of what the candle represents? Is it a momentary, sputtering, flickering light soon to go out if, in fact, it ever flickered in the first place? Or has it a bright, firm, and enduring quality?

Ask yourself as you watch the candle burn, what you have done to strengthen and buttress your faith, what is your relationship to the Maccabean revolt, to the refusal to permit any defilement of our holiest goals.

Ask yourself what more there is you can do. Ask yourself if you really want to make the effort. Ask yourself whether it is worth the candle.

I. Edward Kiev

Actions, Not Words

THOUGHTS OF COMFORT

I. Edward Kiev

PATIENCE

In Judaism, God waits for man to repent; God is a God who waits. We recite the prayer "Thou art slow to anger and ready to forgive. Thou desirest not the death of the sinner but that he return from his evil ways and live. Even until his dying day Thou waitest for him. If he repents Thou wilt immediately receive him."

When we stop to reflect on this, it is rather a striking thought. We usually think of a God who does things promptly and swiftly. He has only to will things and they happen. But the prayer book reminds us that this is not so, that even when God wants very much for something to happen, He has to wait. However much He desires that we live with justice and righteousness and compassion, He must wait until you and I choose to live this way.

The more we understand the world in which we live, the more impressive becomes the evidence that God is a God who waits. In less sophisticated times it was generally believed that when God wanted man to appear, He simply mixed a few elements and before the sun had set, man had arisen. Today we know otherwise. Slowly, painfully, over thousands and perhaps millions of years, man evolved from his primeval form until he could stand erect and look toward the heavens. God was in no hurry when He made man. First, He fashioned the impulse to life in a one-celled protozoa, and then He waited.

Wherever we look we find very little evidence that God is ever in a great hurry. On the contrary, everything we see indicates patience and planning and waiting. The most delicate flower, the sturdiest tree,

I. Edward Kiev

the tallest mountain, each testifies in its own eloquent way that God knows how to wait.

As we read the remarkable history of our people we notice some of this Divine patience reflected in it. Isben, the great Norwegian playwright, wrote that the Jews taught Him "how to wait." They were driven into Babylonian exile and instead of despairing they waited for decades until the day when they could do what no other people had ever done – go back to the land from which they had been driven.

Several centuries later, they went into exile a second time. Their broken fragments were scattered in every land of the globe. Again they waited – waited for nineteen harsh centuries to be restored to the land which lived in their memories, their rituals, their prayers, and their hopes.

What a remarkable capacity to *wait*. Long, long ago our people affirmed its faith in the day when nations shall beat their swords into plowshares and their spears into pruning hooks, a day when the earth would be covered with justice as the waters cover the sea. And while they saw little evidence of either peace or justice, they nonetheless reaffirmed their faith in the ultimate coming of these things. En route to the gas chambers and the crematoria they repeated Maimondies' declaration of faith, *Ani Maamin*, "I believe in the coming of the Messiah and even though he tarry, nevertheless I will wait for him. I will wait for his coming any day." We are people which has learned supremely the lesson of the Divine, of waiting and hoping without surrendering our hopes.

Each of us needs this ability to wait. So much of our lives is spent waiting. We wait for ambitions to be

Actions, Not Words

filled and dreams to be realized. We wait for loved ones to come back and for the long hard winter to pass. We wait for our hurts to be healed and our sorrows to be softened. "He that can have patience," said Benjamin Franklin, "can have what he wills."

Yet waiting is not popular these days. We are accustomed to speed. Everything must be instant. There's a cute cartoon I remember where a lady in the supermarket looks at a jar of coffee and says, "I think it's misleading to call it instant coffee when you still have to boil the water."

One shrewd observer of life today called attention to some of the verbs we use to describe our daily actions. We leap out of bed, we gulp our coffee, we bolt our food, we whiz downtown, dash into the office, tear our way home, and we drop dead. This is a generation which wants what it wants when it wants it. We want it yesterday, today at the very latest, certainly not tomorrow. We have become worshippers of speed. We become impatient if we miss one turn of the revolving door. Knowing how to wait is not one of our conspicuous qualities.

And that is why we have to be reminded that God is a God who waits. We are descendants of a people which taught humanity how to wait and we ourselves need desperately to know how to wait if we are to achieve some of life's most abiding rewards.

But there is also the problem of waiting too long. Many wait too long to find their way back to the synagogue and to Jewish values; our lives, in the meantime, become depleted of spiritual content. We have to avoid this estrangement between ourselves and our heritage, or loyalties which should grow deeper

I. Edward Kiev

may begin to decay; bonds which should be stronger begin to dissolve.

We often wait too long to do what must be done today in a world which only gives us one day at a time, without any assurance of tomorrow. Our days are so few we frequently lament, and yet we procrastinate as though we had an endless supply.

We wait too long to show kindness. We wait too long to be charitable. A rich man once said, "Why is everybody always criticizing me for being miserly, when everyone knows I have made provision to leave everything I possess to charity when I die?"

We wait too long to be parents to our children – putting off spending time together until economic pressures will be fewer and other obligations less insistent – forgetting how briefly they are children, how swiftly life urges them on and away. We wait too long to speak the words of forgiveness that must be spoken, to set aside the hatreds that should be banished, to read the books that are waiting to be read, to utter prayers which our hearts prompt us to sound, to see the beauty there is to be seen, to hear the music which is here to be heard, to seek repentance which is within reach, to show the love that may no longer be needed tomorrow, to do now what we may not be able to do next year.

A persistent attitude in our career as an eternal people, an attitude that is not frequently pointed out or discussed, is our strangely unique habit of conducting debates with God. We talk to Him. We disagree with Him. We demand justice when we think we were unjustly treated. Our first ancestor, you will remember, argued with God about sparing Sodom and Gomorrah. Job has a tremendous argument with God. We are familiar with the great Hasidic outpourings commonly called the *Din Torah* with God.

As we conclude this festival we also conclude the reading of the fifth book of the Torah. Moses persistently argues with God, asking God for justice. He tells the people, "I pleaded with God at that time `O Lord, let me cross the Jordan. Let me enter the promised land."

On the whole, it looks like a just claim. Moses worked hard to deliver the people; first, when he stood before Pharaoh, then on the hard journey with them through the wilderness. The people rebelled often, constantly grumbling, sometimes practicing idolatry: but he managed to overcome many hard times and brought them closer and closer to the promised land. Finally, almost at the shores of the Jordan, Moses is forbidden to complete the arduous task. He wants to know why he must die before finishing the great mission entrusted to him. God said to him "*Rav Lecho.*" That is enough now. God silenced him, stopped any discussion.

In this way God wanted to indicate that his desire to finish his work is not possible. Little tasks can be begun, continued and finished, but the great tasks, the world's work, is never finished. God said to him, in effect, do you think your job will be done if I let you cross the Jordan and go into the promised land? You received from me the Ten Commandments at Sinai. Have those commandments been obeyed? Is that task of establishing law and order completed anywhere in the whole world? You are the first prophet, you will

I. Edward Kiev

have many successors. Among them, Isaiah, who said, "the lion will lie down peaceably. A little child shall lead them." Has that work been finished? When will the world be in perfect peace? *Rav Lecho.* Stop. Thine is not the duty to complete the task, but neither are thou free to desist from it."

Actions, Not Words

DEATH

Hallowed memories crowd in upon us as we approach the fact of death. So has it been since man first reflected on the lives of his dear ones whom he had lived to see die. For the pain of death and the agony of parting are to be found not in the experience of he who dies, but in the heart of the bereaved. Our thoughts turn to those who were and now are not, to those who breathed and now are silent, to those who moved and now are still. Again we live through those first trying hours of life without them, that poignant, inexpressible sentiment which pervades body and soul before time began its healing.

With profound reason this service is called Yizkor, Memorial Service. Through the power of memory we recall the lives and deeds of those no longer with us.

Not through some magical process, not through conjury or necromancy do we seek to call them back, but through a remembrance of impressions, a recognition of the influence our dear ones had upon us and upon the world. It would not be worthy of this moment solely to awaken grief again. It has never been the purpose of Judaism to renew the wound caused by the angel's sword, nor to remind us of the anguish we knew when death kissed the lips of the beloved. Rather, this moment is a reminder to us that we, too, are mortal; that even as in our memory those who preceded us live again, so too in time shall we be a memory to those who follow us; that those who remember others are, in turn, remembered.

We grow so certain of ourselves, so sure of our powers so proud of our creations that we tend to forget

I. Edward Kiev

our mortal status. This hour would remind us that though we climb the heights of achievement, fly high into the skies of attainment, garner wealth and power, all of these pass away when our eyes are closed and our lips are stilled.

Our fame is spoken of only by the mouths of others; our glory remains only in the memory of those we leave behind. Consider the countless eons that the earth has known and the millions of men and women who have lived within them; old and young, rich and poor, mighty and weak, saint and sinner. Wherein lies their immortality but that we remember them and their works? What remains of them but the words which they uttered, the deeds they performed, the contributions they made, the jobs and sorrows they shared with others? In this way do we recall a Moses and Isaiah and a Hillel, a mother and father, wife or husband, child, sister or brother.

As surely as we laid them to rest in the warmth of the earth, so in our loving memories they are cherished. Yea, even in this quiet hour we feel their presence, hear their voices, know them to be near. Time and distance, even death, have lost their meaning; our departed live again with us, and in us they have their being.

Within this hour, then, as we recall our beloved departed, may we recognize the challenge given to us – so to live, so to act, even so to die, that our memorial be an ever-lasting remembrance for good. For the essence of immortality is memory; in death, even as in life, "the righteous lives by his faith."

There are hours of great loneliness, when the frost of desolation penetrates into the very soul, when the

Actions, Not Words

burden seems too heavy to bear, and the draught of life too bitter to swallow. But the very keenness of the ordeal begets the strength to bear it, and patience and unselfish resignation will come as with the rustling of angel's wings to dry our scalding tears.

I. Edward Kiev

COURAGE

Perhaps the primary distinction of a courageous person is how he reacts to the state of being alone. Most of us are not compelled to linger with the knowledge of our aloneness, for it is a knowledge that can paralyze. There are many tasks to be done in the struggle to earn a livelihood, in the daily work of the businessman, the professional man, the housewife, the teacher, the artist, the craftsman which cannot be done alone. But the conquest of material things is not man's only duty. He must also conquer the great wilderness of himself, in the recesses of his own soul. It is for each of us to illuminate that darkness which surrounds us, to make our world a better and brighter dwelling place. The aloneness we feel now is much like the fear of aloneness we sometimes see in the eyes of someone who is suffering, whom we cannot help. The states of birth, suffering, love and death are extreme states – extreme, universal, and inescapable.

To cope, we turn to our ancient faith to find solace for our suffering and pain as we try to rediscover the mystery of life and death, to know that visible reality hides greater reality in the things unseen. Courage is the strongest virtue we need in times such as this. It is a virtue we would wish our children and grandchildren to possess, a quality of mind and heart which can enrich the life experience of young and old alike.

Webster's Dictionary regards it as "that quality of mind which enables one to encounter danger and difficulties with firmness." Ralph Waldo Emerson said that "the courageous man is no braver than any

Actions, Not Words

ordinary man but he is braver five minutes longer." And the poet, John Donne suggested that a courageous man is one who performs a brave deed and does not tell anyone about it.

However we may choose to define it, courage is a badge of honor we should all strive to claim for ourselves.

Printed in the United States
755200001B